COPYRIGHT

THIS BOOK BELONGS TO

_____

WHO WANTS TO BECOME

A/AN_____

BY (enter date) _____

STUDENT'S SIGNATURE_____

DATE SIGNED _____

PARENT'S/GUARDIAN'S SIGNATURE_____

DATE SIGNED_____

www.mycheetahacademy.com

CHEETAH™ Toys & More, LLC Copyright 2022 © Copying is NOT allowed

CHEETAH™
Connect to **H**igher **E**ducation, **E**lectronic **T**ools, **A**plication and **H**elp

COPYRIGHT

10 9 8 7 6 5 4 3 2

Copyright© 2022. All rights reserved.

No part of this publication may be reproduced, distributed, or transmitted in any form or by any means, including photocopying, recording, or other electronic or mechanical methods, without the prior written permission of the publisher, except in the case of brief quotations embodied in critical reviews and certain other non-commercial uses permitted by copyright law.

Although every precaution has been taken to verify the accuracy of the information contained herein, the authors and publisher assume no responsibility for any errors or omissions. No liability is assumed for damages that may result from the use of information contained within. Your legal remedy, if any, is limited to the amount paid for this book and/or training.

ISBN-13: 978-1-7328369-1-4
ISBN-10: 1-7328369-1-4

Permission request(s) should be submitted to the publisher in writing at one of the addresses below:

CHEETAH® Toys & More, LLC
207 Main Street, 4th Floor
Hartford, CT 06106

Port Antonio PO
Portland, Jamaica
info@mycheetahacademy.com
paulettetrowers@yahoo.com
WhatsApp: 876-909-6311

Authors: Paulette Trowers, JD and a team of educators
Editors: Bernadette Vidal and Fiona Porter-Lawson
Cover and Interior Design: CHEETAH® Purrrrrrr Publishing ('CHEETAH®'), an imprint of CHEETAH® Toys & More, LLC.
Publisher: CHEETAH® (**C**onnect to **H**igher **E**ducation, **E**lectronic **T**ools, **A**pplication & **H**elp)

ACKNOWLEDGEMENTS

Thanks to the many people who reviewed and/or provided feedback. CHEETAH® appreciates your effort. We are so glad that you share our company's mission and vision for our Jamaican educational system and students.

www.mycheetahacademy.com

CHEETAH™ Toys & More, LLC Copyright 2022 © Copying is NOT allowed

CONTENT

Table of contents

Honour system 3

Dear CHEETAH family 4

PEP ability test key concepts 7

CHEETAH® 40-Questions tests 21

   40-QUESTIONS TEST #1 24
   40-QUESTIONS TEST #2 40
   40-QUESTIONS TEST #3 54
   40-QUESTIONS TEST #4 66
   40-QUESTIONS TEST #5 82
   40-QUESTIONS TEST #6 98
   40-QUESTIONS TEST #7 114
   40-QUESTIONS TEST #8 130
   40-QUESTIONS TEST #9 148

Answers and explanations 157

   40-QUESTIONS TEST #1 Answer key 158
   40-QUESTIONS TEST #2 Answer key 164
   40-QUESTIONS TEST #3 Answer key 171
   40-QUESTIONS TEST #4 Answer key 178
   40-QUESTIONS TEST #5 Answer key 184
   40-QUESTIONS TEST #6 Answer key 191
   40-QUESTIONS TEST #7 Answer key 197

CONTENT

40-QUESTIONS TEST #8 Answer key..205

40-QUESTIONS TEST #9 Answer key..212

I am LaChase, the cheetah. I will educate, entertain and inspire you! Come wid mi. Grab some confidence along the way! Why?

'If you have no confidence in self you are twice defeated in the race of life. With confidence you have won even before you have started.'
Marcus Garvey

CHEETAH'S™ HONOUR SYSTEM PLEDGE

Honour system

You will notice that this workbook includes the answers for most, if not all, of the questions. We are providing you with these answer keys based on the **honour system**, which is closely associated with having a **conscience**. We trust you to act honestly, even though no one is monitoring you.

Take our CHEETAH® **honour system pledge** today!

CHEETAH'S
Honour system pledge

I, _____,

of _____

school, Grade _____, located at _____

_____,

agree to abide by the honour system, as explained in this book.

Signed:_____

Dated:_____

Witnessed by:_____

www.mycheetahacademy.com

CHEETAH™ Toys & More, LLC Copyright 2022 © Copying is NOT allowed

3

CHEETAH™
Connect to Higher Education, Electronic Tools, Aplication and Help

ABOUT THIS BOOK

Dear CHEETAH family,

Welcome to the CHEETAH® PEP Ability Practice Questions Workbook. The goal of this workbook is to improve your critical thinking skills and help you prepare for the upcoming PEP Ability Exam. We are therefore providing a complete guide and a practical tool for students, teachers and parents.

We will follow our **CHEETAH CAPE** © principle in four easy steps.

1. We want you to **C - comprehend** the concept, that is, the rule, key principle or big idea related to a specific topic.

2. You will **A -apply** your knowledge of the concepts by working on some examples.

3. We will allow you to **P- practise** on your own by completing the tests.

4. We ask that you occasionally **E - evaluate** your work or ask someone to evaluate it for you.

ABOUT THIS BOOK

This workbook is packed with interesting features that will enhance the learning experience. These include:

1. key concepts
2. peer review sessions
3. 40-questions tests
4. answers and explanations
5. CHEETAH® top tips
6. curriculum drivers
7. special assignments

You are encouraged to write in this workbook and review the contents multiple times while preparing for the PEP ability test.

ABOUT THIS BOOK

Let's go!
Let's go!
Let's prep for PEP and life!

PEP ability test key concepts

KEY CONCEPTS

Ability tests: What are they and how do I pass them?

Ability tests are designed to assess your power to think! They feature different types of questions and problems. You will not have specific content to study. Instead, you must use **reasoning skills**, work out rules, and establish relationships and structures to choose the correct answer from a set of four options. The goal of every question is the same — to **assess your understanding and ability** to make the right decision.

On the day of your Primary Exit Profile (PEP) ability test, you will be given 40 multiple-choice questions to complete in 1 hour and 30 minutes. For each question, there will be four possible answers. You must choose the correct answer or answers. Please read the instructions carefully.

These questions will NOT be based on specific content but will focus on reasoning skills. **So, how will you know what will be on the exam?**

According to the Ministry of Education and Youth (MOEY), the ability test will:

> 'assess students' aptitude in areas of numeracy, verbal and non-verbal reasoning, and abstract thinking abilities and requires students to read analytically and demonstrate quantitative reasoning skills.'

Based on the description and the sample questions that the Ministry provided, we believe that the questions on the ability test COULD include logical reasoning questions that are verbal and non-verbal.

Let us review what these categories mean.

KEY CONCEPTS

Ability tests: Question types

Logical Reasoning Questions
test your ability to follow a set of rules to solve a problem.

Verbal Reasoning Questions
test your ability to understand and reason with words.

Non-Verbal Reasoning Questions
test your ability to solve problems which do not involve the use of language.

Numeracy Questions
test your ability to solve problems which require you to use, explain or untangle mathematical information.

Analytical Questions
test your ability to methodically examine and interpret data to answer a question or solve a problem.

Abstract Reasoning Questions
test your ability to understand and reason with visual information.

Quantitative Reasoning Questions
test your ability to analyse numerical data to solve problems.

Confucius said that 'a journey of a thousand miles begins with a single step.' You and I are readers and leaders who are chasing and capturing our educational goals one step at a time. Let's go. Let's prep for PEP and life.

KEY CONCEPTS

Ability tests: Question examples overview

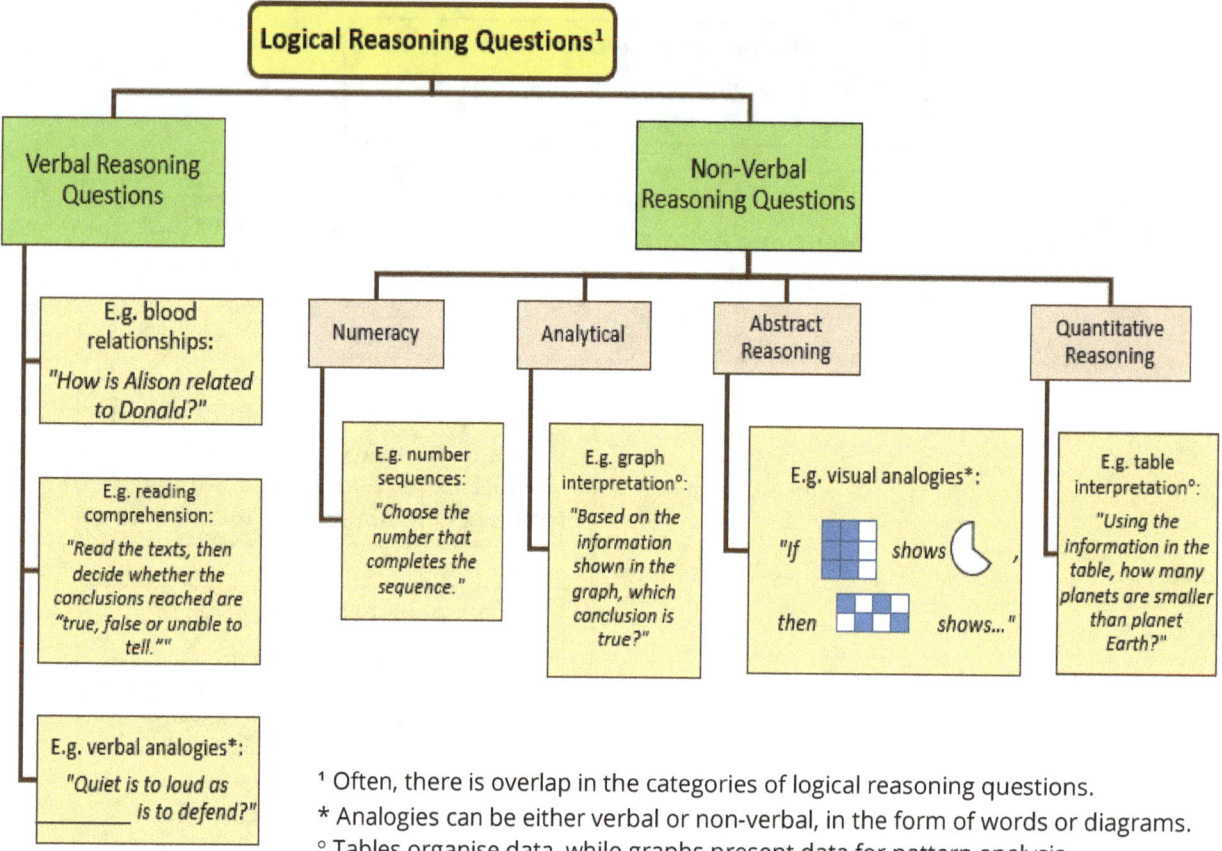

[1] Often, there is overlap in the categories of logical reasoning questions.
* Analogies can be either verbal or non-verbal, in the form of words or diagrams.
° Tables organise data, while graphs present data for pattern analysis.

Logical reasoning questions

Logic is a way of thinking that is **reasonable** and uses sound judgement. Using logic helps you to decide if something is true or false. **Logical reasoning** questions test your ability to follow a set of rules to **solve a problem**.

> **CHEETAH® TOP TIP!**
>
> Practice makes perfect! The more you practise logical reasoning questions, the more you will sharpen the skills required to reach the correct conclusion.

It is often best to try to figure out the solution *before* you look at the answer options. If you have applied logic to reach an answer which is an option, you can be confident it is correct. Trickier questions may require you to start with the answers and eliminate those which are impossible. This can help you to arrive at the correct answer. This is known as using a **process of elimination**.

KEY CONCEPTS

Verbal reasoning questions

Verbal describes anything related to words. Verbal reasoning questions will therefore test your ability to **solve word problems** in a logical way.

Example: Blood relationships

Questions about **family relationships** are often included on ability tests. The chart below also provides a basis from which to use logic to solve blood relationship problems.

> **CHEETAH® TOP TIP!**
>
> Talking to your own family about how everyone is related is a great way to practise blood relationship questions.

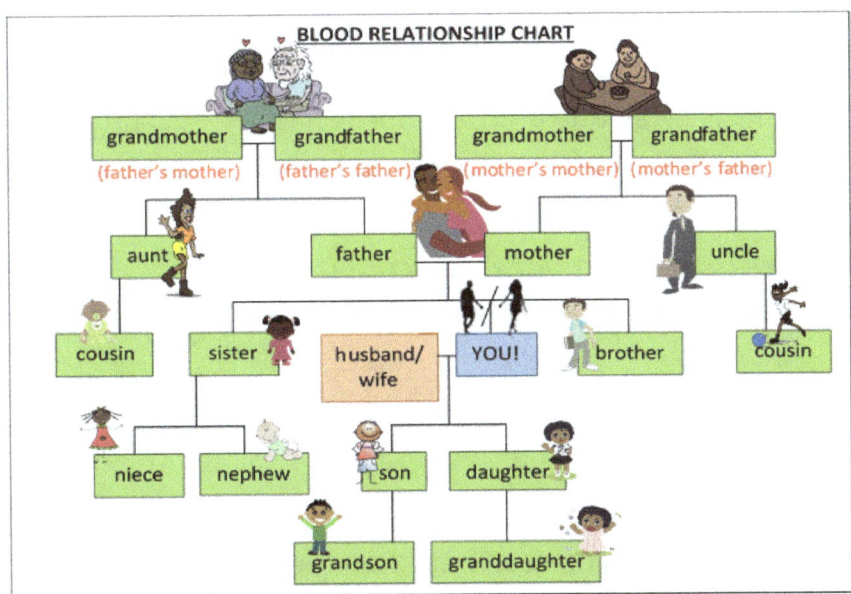

Let's take a look at a question about blood relationships.

Alison is Bridget's sister. Cassie is Bridget's mother. Donald is Cassie's father. Eleanor is Donald's mother. Then, how is Alison related to Donald?
   A. Alison is Donald's grandmother.
   B. Donald is Alison's grandfather.
   C. Alison is Donald's daughter.
   D. Donald is Alison's brother.

Can you **logically decide** how Alison is related to Donald?

1. Let's take the information a step at a time and build a visual picture of the family. First, Alison is Bridget's sister.

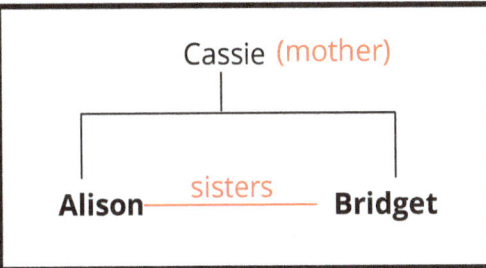

KEY CONCEPTS

2. Next, Cassie is Bridget's mother. As Alison and Bridget are sisters, both girls must be Cassie's children.
3. Donald is Cassie's father, and Eleanor is Donald's mother. We add these relationships to the diagram.
4. If Donald is the father of Alison's mother, he must be Alison's grandfather. The correct answer is therefore option B.

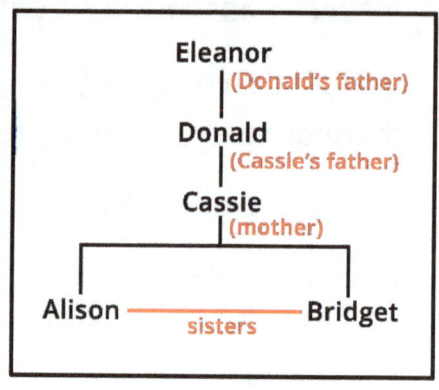

Example: Comprehension

Comprehension questions test your ability to read a passage of text and answer questions about it. The topic of the passage may be a subject you know nothing about. This is to your advantage, as you will be expected to answer the questions based on the information in the text, without relying on any prior knowledge.

CHEETAH® TOP TIP!

Regularly reading a range of texts and playing word games will widen your vocabulary and make verbal reasoning questions much easier to solve.

Using only the information in the passage, you may be asked to evaluate a statement as one of the following:

- **True** – The statement is correct, based on the information in the passage.
- **False** – The statement is incorrect, based on the information in the passage.
- **Partially true** – The statement is partially correct, but not entirely.
- **Unable to tell** – The information in the passage is not enough to decide whether the statement is true or false.

Let's look at a comprehension question.

Below are two boxes, each containing an extract. Read the texts, then decide whether the conclusion reached is 'true, false, partially true or unable to tell.'

> **Extract 1**
>
> Native to Jamaica, the Homerus Swallowtail is the largest species of butterfly found in the Western Hemisphere. A Swedish botanist named many swallowtail butterfly species after Greek figures, including this gigantic insect, which is named after the Greek poet, Homer.
>
> Though a symbol of Jamaican national pride, this species suffers habitat destruction and illegal trade, and is now protected both nationally and internationally.

KEY CONCEPTS

Extract 2

Queen Alexandra's birdwing is an endangered species of butterfly found in the forests of Papua New Guinea. With females boasting a wingspan of up to 30 cm, it is the largest butterfly in the world. This butterfly was discovered by an English natural history specimen collector, who shot the first specimen down with a shotgun! Later specimens were bred from caterpillars and chrysalides.

The Homerus Swallowtail is the second largest species of butterfly in the world.

- **A.** true
- **B.** false
- **C.** partially true
- **D.** unable to tell

> **CHEETAH® TOP TIP!**
>
> Do not make assumptions! Base your conclusions only on the information given.

To evaluate the statements, we will need to look for evidence in the passages.

A. Extract 2 describes the Queen Alexandra's birdwing as 'the largest butterfly in the world.' This suggests that it is possible that the Homerus Swallowtail *could* be the second largest.

B. Looking for further evidence in Extract 1, the Homerus Swallowtail is the 'largest species of butterfly found in the Western Hemisphere' and is 'gigantic.' But who is to say that there is not another species of butterfly, outside of the Western Hemisphere, that is bigger than the Homerus Swallowtail but smaller than the Queen Alexandra's birdwing?

C. As we cannot conclude whether the statement is true or false, we must give the answer 'unable to tell' for the statement that 'The Homerus Swallowtail is the second largest species of butterfly in the world.'

Example: Verbal analogies

An analogy compares two largely different things that have something in common. These questions test your ability to recognise relationships between pairs of words. Once you have worked out the relationship, you can use this information to deduce the correct option for a word missing its partner.

Here are some common types of word relationship that may be presented to you:

KEY CONCEPTS

Analogy type	Explanation	Example
Antonyms	The two words are opposites.	*Hot is to cold as night is to day.*
Synonyms	The two words have a similar meaning.	*True is to correct as happiness is to joy.*
Cause and effect	One word is the reason that the other word has happened.	*Tired is to yawn as itch is to scratch.*
Part and whole	One word is a part of the whole represented by the other.	*Page is to book as feather is to bird.*
Category and example	One word is an example of something which fits the category described by the other.	*Spoon is to cutlery as iguana is to reptile.*

Ready to take a look at a question?

Quiet is to loud as _____ is to defend.

    A. shout
    B. stand
    C. attack
    D. block

Here is a suggested strategy:

1. Spot the relationship between the words. You should reach the conclusion that *quiet* and *loud* are antonyms, which means they have opposite meanings.

   Presented with the answer options A. *shout*, B. *stand*, C. *attack* and D. *block*, you need to decide which is the **antonym** for *defend*. Option C. *attack* has the **opposite meaning** to *defend* and so would be the correct answer to the problem.

Non-verbal reasoning questions

Non-verbal describes anything not relating to words. Non-verbal reasoning questions will therefore test your ability to solve problems which do not focus on words. These include numeracy, analytical reasoning, **abstract reasoning** and quantitative reasoning questions. Let's take a look at each of these types.

KEY CONCEPTS

Numeracy questions

Numeracy is the ability to understand and use numbers. Numeracy questions test your ability to solve problems which require you to use, explain or figure out mathematical information, often requiring addition, subtraction, division and multiplication skills. You may also need to understand probability, fractions, decimals and percentages to answer other types of numeracy questions.

> **CHEETAH® TOP TIP!**
>
> Practising your multiplication tables will make it easier and quicker to solve problems requiring multiplication and division skills.

Example: Number sequences

You may be asked to choose the correct number to complete a sequence. In order to do this, you must first think about the rules the sequence follows, then use these rules to work out which number comes next.

Look at this question.

Choose the number that completes the following sequence:

10, 22, 35, 49, 64, _?

A. 71   B. 75   C. 79   D. 80

Can you spot the rule that the numbers are following?

1. To move from 10 to 22, 12 has been added to the number 10. To move from 22 to 35, 13 is added to the number 22. Do you see the pattern?

2. First 12 was added and then 13, so perhaps 14 will be added next time. 35 + 14 = 49, which fits the rule!

3. Continuing the rule along the sequence, 49 + 15 = 64, so the next number in the sequence must follow suit... 64 + 16 = 80. The answer is therefore D. 80.

Analytical reasoning questions

Analytical reasoning requires looking into the details of things to find out more. You must separate a bigger picture into parts and examine each element in a logical, critical way.

KEY CONCEPTS

Analytical reasoning questions will ask you to **examine and interpret data** to answer a question or solve a problem. These questions may also be referred to as numeric or quantitative reasoning problems if the data involved is numbers.

Example: Graph interpretation

You may be asked to interpret data presented in a chart to reach a conclusion. This could be a line graph, a bar chart, a pie chart, a **table**, or a graph you may never have seen before! In each case, carefully consider all the information shown; read the question carefully, read the graph and axes titles, understand how the data has been plotted, before correctly interpreting the data to select the correct answer.

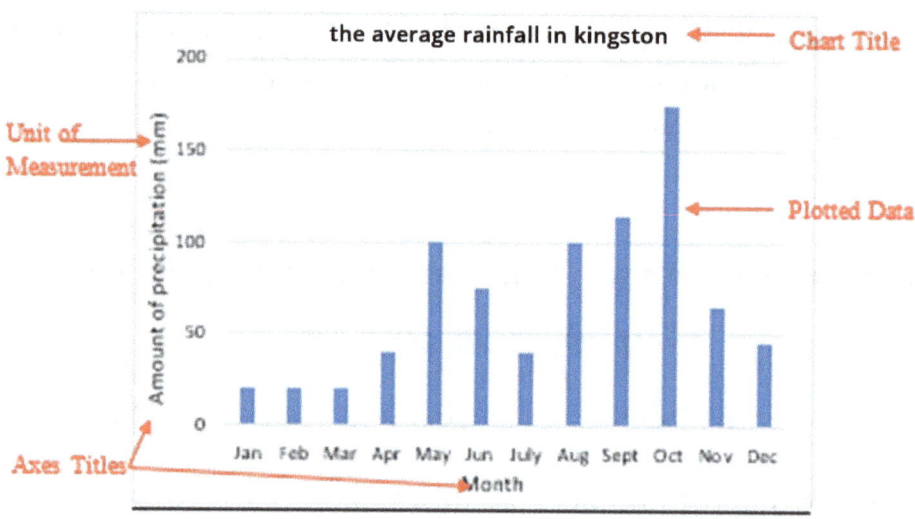

Look at the graph that follows this question. It shows an ice cream stall's sale of different flavours over four weeks.

Based on the information shown in the graph, which conclusion is true?

    A. Strawberry was the least popular flavour over the four-week period.
    B. The ice cream seller sold more than 400 ice creams over the four-week period.
    C. Chocolate was the most popular flavour over the four-week period.
    D. The sales of vanilla ice cream steadily increased over the four-week period.

KEY CONCEPTS

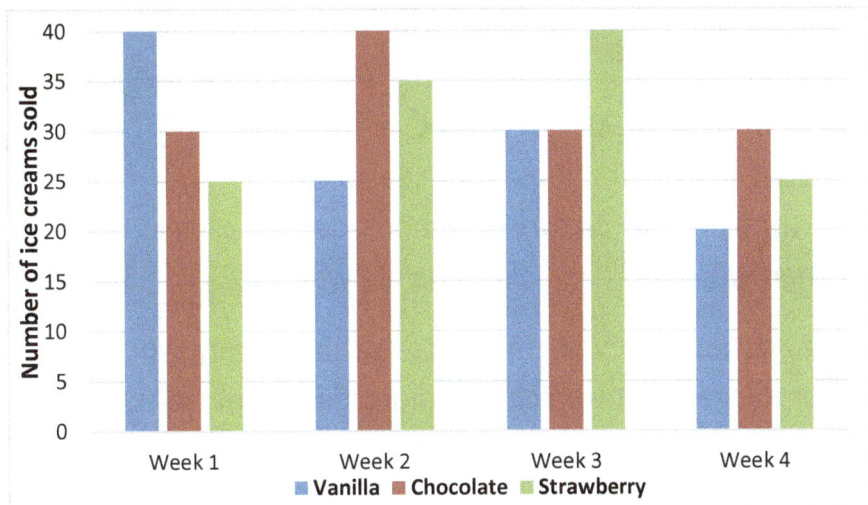

Have you read the axis titles and the legend on the graph? Can you see what data is required to check whether each statement is true or false?

1. Each statement will need to be carefully considered. For statement A, you must add the sales of each flavour of ice cream over the four-week period. In week 1, 40 vanilla ice creams were sold, 25 in week 2, 30 in week 3 and 20 in week 4. 40+25+30+20 = 115 vanilla ice creams sold in 4 weeks.
   For chocolate, 30+40+30+30 = 130 sold. Finally, strawberry sales were 35+35+40+25, which equals 125 sold altogether. As ten more strawberry ice creams were sold compared to vanilla, strawberry was NOT the least popular flavour, and statement A is false.

2. To verify statement B, you will need to add ALL the ice cream sales to find the total over the four-week period. You already know that the sales totals were 115 vanilla, 130 chocolate, and 125 strawberry. Adding these gives a total of 370 ice creams sold, which is LESS than 400. Statement B is therefore also false.

3. For statement C, you already have the answers to the calculations required. Chocolate sales were 130 ice creams in total, compared to 125 strawberry and 115 vanilla. With the most sales, chocolate was indeed the most popular flavour over the four-week period, and statement C is true.

4. Checking statement D will confirm you have the correct answer. Vanilla sales will need to have increased a little week on week. However, from a high number of sales in week 1 (40), sales dropped to 25 ice creams in week 2, increased to 30 in week 3, then dropped again in week 4 to 20. Statement D is therefore also false.

5. With all statements carefully analysed, you can be confident that the correct answer is C. Chocolate was the most popular flavour over the four-week period.

KEY CONCEPTS

Abstract reasoning questions

Abstract describes a thought or idea that is often represented by shapes or colours. **Abstract** reasoning is the action of thinking of pictures, shapes and diagrams (rather than words) in a logical, sensible way.

> **CHEETAH® TOP TIP!**
> Looking for repetition of colour, shape or size can help you to notice a pattern.

Abstract reasoning questions will therefore often present you with pictures or diagrams, shapes or images, from which you must identify patterns and rules to solve problems.

Example: Analogies

As you were presented with a verbal analogy, you may also be presented with an analogy that is visual. In this case, you will be asked to recognise relationships between images. The key to solving a **visual analogy** is to look at the images carefully, understand what you see, and recognise the relationship or rule that connects the pair. This relationship can then be applied to selecting another pair's missing partner correctly.

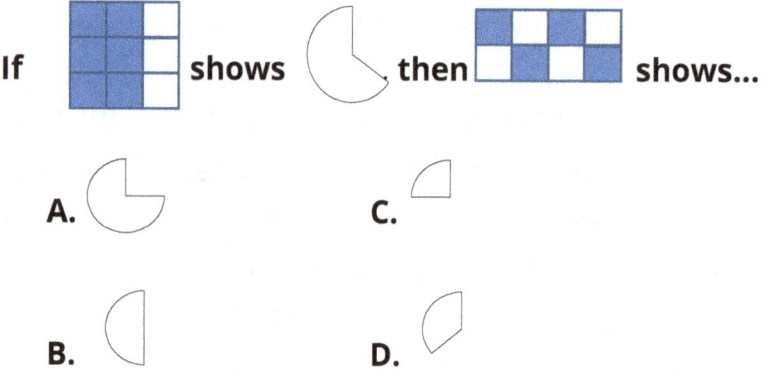

Can you see a relationship between the grid and the pie? Use this relationship to work out the missing partner for the second grid.

1. If you think of the shapes as representing fractions, you will see that 6 squares of 9 are blue in the first grid, which can be simplified to two thirds.

2. Two-thirds is also represented by the pie proportion it has been paired with, so the fractions represented are the same!

KEY CONCEPTS

3. Using this information, the fraction represented by the second grid can be calculated: 4 squares of 8 have been shaded blue, which simplifies to one half. Option B shows half of a pie—the equivalent fraction and the correct answer.

Quantitative reasoning questions

Quantitative refers to an amount that expresses a quantity or a measurement. **Quantitative reasoning questions** test your ability to analyse numerical data to solve problems. These questions can include graphs, charts and tables for you to interpret, which are often testing your analytical reasoning skills too!

> **CHEETAH® TOP TIP!**
> Double check you have found all the numbers you need from the table before settling on your answer to the problem.

EXAMPLE: Tables

A **table** displays information, or data, in rows and columns. It is important to understand the context or background of the data. You can do this by carefully reading any information before or after the table. The column headings are also key to understanding what the words and numbers mean.

Look at this question.

The table below shows information about the eight planets in our solar system.

Planet	Distance from sun (million km)	Diameter (km)	Number of confirmed moons
Earth	149.6	12,756	1
Jupiter	778.4	142,984	53
Mars	227.9	6,794	2
Mercury	57.9	4,879	0
Neptune	4498.3	49,528	14
Saturn	1426.7	120,536	53
Uranus	2871.0	51,118	27
Venus	108.2	12,104	0

KEY CONCEPTS

**Use the information in the table to answer the following question.
How many planets are smaller than planet Earth?**

         A. 1   B. 2   C. 3   D. 4

Can you see which column displays the data you need for this question?

1. The question concerns the size of the planets, so you will first need to establish which part of the table contains the information you need. The planets' names are listed in the first column, so this column will be important in solving the question.

2. The second column tells you the distance of each planet from the sun, while the fourth column lists the number of each planet's moons. Both subjects are irrelevant to the question you have been asked.

3. It is therefore the third column, with the title 'diameter' that holds the information needed to solve the problem. Your mathematical knowledge will confirm that the word diameter refers to the distance across the centre of a sphere, so these numbers give information about each planet's size.

4. By finding 'Earth' in the first column and following the row across to the 'diameter' column, you will see that the distance across the centre of our planet is 12,756 km.

5. As the question asks how many planets are smaller than Earth, you will need to look for numbers in the 'diameter' column that are less than 12,756. There are three numbers less than 12,756: 6,794; 4,879 and 12,104.

6. As there are three planets with smaller diameters than planet Earth, the correct answer is option C: 3.

Let us **A** - apply your knowledge.
Ready to **P** - practise? Let's go!
Let's prep for PEP and life!

CHEETAH® 40-QUESTIONS TESTS

'Success is never final and failure never fatal. It's courage that counts.'
—GEORGE F. TILTON—

40-QUESTIONS TEST #1
ANSWER SHEET

The next page has an answer sheet that you will use to record your answers. It is like the one you will most likely use during your PEP exams. Please remove this page.

(OPTIONAL HELPFUL INFORMATION)

TEST #: _____

START TIME: _____

END TIME:_____

SCORE:_____

'We are what we repeatedly do. Excellence, then, is not an act but a habit.'

– ARISTOTLE–

Start this test whenever you are told to do so or whenever you are ready.

40-QUESTIONS TEST #1

Name: _____ ID no. _____ Age: ___

School: _____ School address: _____

1	Ⓐ	Ⓑ	Ⓒ	Ⓓ	21	Ⓐ	Ⓑ	Ⓒ	Ⓓ
2	Ⓐ	Ⓑ	Ⓒ	Ⓓ	22	Ⓐ	Ⓑ	Ⓒ	Ⓓ
3	Ⓐ	Ⓑ	Ⓒ	Ⓓ	23	Ⓐ	Ⓑ	Ⓒ	Ⓓ
4	Ⓐ	Ⓑ	Ⓒ	Ⓓ	24	Ⓐ	Ⓑ	Ⓒ	Ⓓ
5	Ⓐ	Ⓑ	Ⓒ	Ⓓ	25	Ⓐ	Ⓑ	Ⓒ	Ⓓ
6	Ⓐ	Ⓑ	Ⓒ	Ⓓ	26	Ⓐ	Ⓑ	Ⓒ	Ⓓ
7	Ⓐ	Ⓑ	Ⓒ	Ⓓ	27	Ⓐ	Ⓑ	Ⓒ	Ⓓ
8	Ⓐ	Ⓑ	Ⓒ	Ⓓ	28	Ⓐ	Ⓑ	Ⓒ	Ⓓ
9	Ⓐ	Ⓑ	Ⓒ	Ⓓ	29	Ⓐ	Ⓑ	Ⓒ	Ⓓ
10	Ⓐ	Ⓑ	Ⓒ	Ⓓ	30	Ⓐ	Ⓑ	Ⓒ	Ⓓ
11	Ⓐ	Ⓑ	Ⓒ	Ⓓ	31	Ⓐ	Ⓑ	Ⓒ	Ⓓ
12	Ⓐ	Ⓑ	Ⓒ	Ⓓ	32	Ⓐ	Ⓑ	Ⓒ	Ⓓ
13	Ⓐ	Ⓑ	Ⓒ	Ⓓ	33	Ⓐ	Ⓑ	Ⓒ	Ⓓ
14	Ⓐ	Ⓑ	Ⓒ	Ⓓ	34	Ⓐ	Ⓑ	Ⓒ	Ⓓ
15	Ⓐ	Ⓑ	Ⓒ	Ⓓ	35	Ⓐ	Ⓑ	Ⓒ	Ⓓ
16	Ⓐ	Ⓑ	Ⓒ	Ⓓ	36	Ⓐ	Ⓑ	Ⓒ	Ⓓ
17	Ⓐ	Ⓑ	Ⓒ	Ⓓ	37	Ⓐ	Ⓑ	Ⓒ	Ⓓ
18	Ⓐ	Ⓑ	Ⓒ	Ⓓ	38	Ⓐ	Ⓑ	Ⓒ	Ⓓ
19	Ⓐ	Ⓑ	Ⓒ	Ⓓ	39	Ⓐ	Ⓑ	Ⓒ	Ⓓ
20	Ⓐ	Ⓑ	Ⓒ	Ⓓ	40	Ⓐ	Ⓑ	Ⓒ	Ⓓ

Score _____ out of 40

40-QUESTIONS TEST #1

For the questions below, choose the word that best finishes the sentence.

1. Light is to day as dark is to _____.

   A. afternoon   B. night   C. morning   D. dawn

2. Pig is to piglets as _____ is to kids.

   A. chicken   B. dog   C. goat   D. cow

3. Dry is to wet as big is to _____.

   A. tall   B. huge   C. fat   D. small

4. Hard is to soft as _____ is to full.

   A. empty   C. finished
   B. overflowing   D. measure

For items 5 and 6, choose the word that is an essential part of the underlined word.

5. <u>book</u>

   A. words   B. pictures   C. blurbs   D. pages

6. <u>music</u>

   A. drum   B. sound   C. singing   D. guitar

For items 7 to 9, choose the word that does not fit the group.

7. A. owl   B. cuckoo   C. pigeon   D. iguana

8. A. dominoes   B. cricket   C. athletics   D. football

9. A. students   B. teachers   C. school   D. parents

Read the passage below before answering items 10 to 12.

The Jamaican Boa is the largest snake on the island of Jamaica, reaching lengths of up to 2.5 m. As the name suggests, this snake cannot be found anywhere else in the world.

In the day, these snakes hide away in dense vegetation but emerge <u>now and again</u> to sunbathe and warm up their bodies. At night, they come out to hunt, using their tongue to detect chemical signals from their prey. Rats, bats, lizards, birds and frogs are ambushed, caught in sharp teeth and then suffocated in the snake's super strong coils before being swallowed whole.

The Jamaican Boa is of no threat to humans, but people continue to fear them, and they are often killed on sight. With their habitat also threatened, they are now considered an <u>endangered species</u> and may become extinct in the wild.

10. _____ means the same as 'now and again'.
  A. always
  B. never
  C. often
  D. sometimes

11. Which of these animals is also considered an indigenous 'endangered species'?
  A. Australian red-claw lobster
  B. small Indian mongoose
  C. long tail hummingbird
  D. lionfish

12. Why has the writer written this passage?
    A. to inform the reader about Jamaican Boas
    B. to inform the reader about Jamaica
    C. to tell the reader to kill Jamaican Boas
    D. to tell the reader to stop killing Jamaican Boas

The steps for making roti are shown in the pictures below.

1

2

3

4

5

13. Which of the following sequences puts the steps of making roti into logical order?

    A. 1, 3, 4, 5, 2
    B. 4, 5, 1, 3, 2
    C. 2, 3, 5, 1, 4
    D. 3, 5, 1, 4, 2

14. Choose the right option to complete the sequence.
    egg, tadpole, froglet, _____
    A. frog
    B. larva
    C. pupa
    D. iguana

15. Look closely at the words in the box, then choose the logical sequence.

> wood   book
>
>   tree   paper

   A. wood, paper, book, tree
   B. tree, wood, paper, book
   C. paper, book, tree, wood
   D. tree, paper, wood, book

16. Maria is older than Tommy. Johnny is older than Maria. Tommy is older than Johnny. If the first two sentences are true, then the third one is:
   A. true
   B. false
   C. uncertain
   D. partially true

For items 17 to 19, choose the best word to complete each statement.

17. People who _____ have stronger muscles and bones.
   A. read
   B. steal
   C. exercise
   D. wash

18. An island is _____ by water.
   A. followed
   B. surrounded
   C. identified
   D. measured

19. Gabriel went to _____ eggs to cook for breakfast.
    A. by
    B. bye
    C. buoy
    D. buy

Below are two boxes, each containing an extract. Read the texts, then decide whether the conclusions reached in items 20 and 21 are true, false, partially true, or unable to tell.

Extract 1

The national flag of Jamaica is the only flag in the world that has no colours in common with the flag of the United States of America (USA).

Originally, the flag was designed with three horizontal stripes, but this was too similar to the flag of Tanganyika.

The gold cross we see today represents the country's wealth. The green sections are for the lush vegetation of the island, and the black triangles symbolise the strength of the people who have overcome past difficulties.

Extract 2

Mauritania is a country in Northwest Africa. Much of Mauritania's land is in the Sahara Desert, so most people live in the south where there is more rain.

The flag of Mauritania has a green background with red stripes at the top and bottom. A gold crescent and star in the centre represent the country's state religion of Islam, as well as the golden sands of the Saharan desert.

20. The flag of Mauritania has one or more colours in common with the USA flag.
    A. true
    B. false
    C. partially true
    D. unable to tell

21. The vegetation in Mauritania is less lush than the vegetation in Jamaica.
    A. true
    B. false
    C. partially true
    D. unable to tell

22. Choose the number that completes the following sequence:

    11, 16, 26, 31, 41, 46, _____

    A. 52
    B. 56
    C. 51
    D. 61

23. Each diagram below contains numbers that follow the same rule. Use the information in the first three diagrams to work out the missing number in the last diagram.

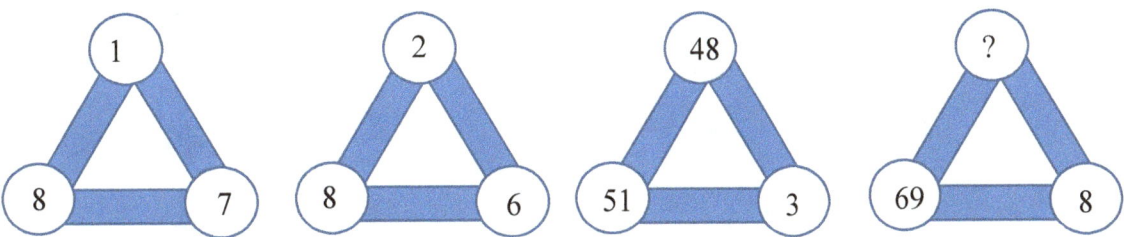

    A. 16
    B. 61
    C. 51
    D. 39

24. Look at the pattern shown below. Use the first two pairs to work out the missing number in the square of the third pair.

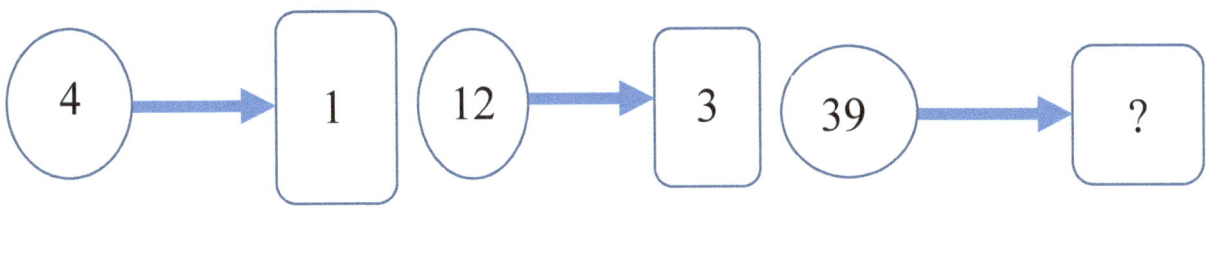

    A. 12
    B. 9
    C. 3
    D. 2

Look at the shapes in the box below. Selena has shown the shapes on a chart.

I.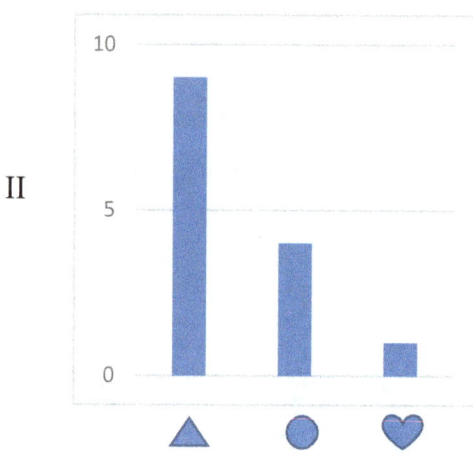

II.

III.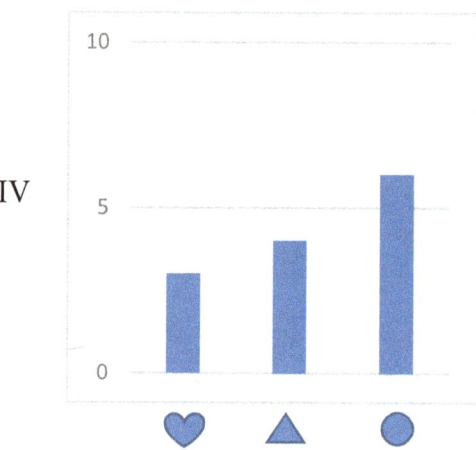

IV.

25. Which chart shows the information correctly?
   A. chart I
   B. chart II
   C. chart III
   D. chart IV

In a survey, 60 grade six students were asked about their favourite athletic events.

- Fewer than 20 students chose throwing events.
- More than half of the students chose running events.
- The same number of students chose jumping events as those who chose throwing events.

26. Which chart shows the information correctly?
    A. chart I
    B. chart II
    C. chart III
    D. chart IV

27. If ▦ shows ◇ then ▦ shows...

A. (circle with small wedge removed)

B. (circle with larger wedge removed)

C. (circle with quarter removed)

D. (half circle)

28. Victoria is 2 years younger than Joshua. Dominic is twice as old as Joshua and Raheem is the oldest. Which is the correct order of the children by age, from youngest to oldest?
    A. Dominic, Raheem, Victoria, Joshua
    B. Victoria, Raheem, Joshua, Dominic
    C. Joshua, Victoria, Dominic, Raheem
    D. Victoria, Joshua, Dominic, Raheem

29. Peter bought a bunch of 10 bananas at the market. Some of the bananas on the bunch were green and the others were yellow. Which of the numbers below could **not** be the number of yellow bananas?
    A. 3
    B. 11
    C. 6
    D. 5

Roseanne has a bag containing the numbers 1 to 10. She takes a number from the bag and performs the operations shown in column A. After that she uses the original number to perform the operations shown in column B.

Column A	Column B
Double the number and then add 2.	Add 10 to the number and then halve it.

30. Using the information given, which of the following option is correct?
    A. The result of column A was the same as the result of column B.
    B. The result of column A was greater than the result of column B.
    C. The result of column A was less than the result of column B.
    D. It is impossible to determine the result based on the information given.

Below is a diagram of a rectangle **EFGH**.

31. Which of the following shows the greatest length?
    A. EF + FG
    B. EG + FH
    C. EF + GH
    D. EF + FH

32. Akilah estimated that there were 25,000 people at the carnival. Of the following numbers, which could **NOT** be the actual number of people at the carnival?
    A. 25,115
    B. 25,462
    C. 24,741
    D. 25,789

40–QUESTIONS TEST #1

33. Jordan is looking for a page in a book. He notices that page 2 is on the right-hand side of the page. When he turns the page over, page 3 is on the left-hand side and faces page 4, on the right. Which of the following pairs of pages will also face each other?
    A. 8 and 9
    B. 12 and 13
    C. 15 and 16
    D. 16 and 17

34. Crystal wants to border one side of her garden with bricks. What information is necessary for her to work out how many bricks she will need?
    A. the area of the garden
    B. the length of the side of the garden
    C. the perimeter of the garden and the length of the bricks
    D. the length of the side of the garden and the length of the bricks

The table below shows the sales of an ice cream shop over a period of 3 days. The information focuses on the sales of three flavours of ice cream, and how much money was made.

Flavour	Day 1		Day 2		Day 3	
	Number of sales	Total made on sales	Number of sales	Total made on sales	Number of sales	Total made on sales
Vanilla	8	$16	22	$44	30	$60
Strawberry	4	$10	14	$35	8	$20
Chocolate chip	3	$9	2	$6	10	$20

Use the information in the table to answer items 35 and 36.

35. On which day did the ice cream shop have the lowest sales?

   A. day 1
   B. day 2
   C. day 3
   D. It is impossible to answer based on the information given.

36. On day 3, the unit price of chocolate chip ice cream changed. What was its price per unit **before** the change?

   A. $2.00
   B. $2.50
   C. $3.00
   D. It is impossible to answer based on the information given.

The diagram below shows how Nicholas spent his time at the beach last weekend.

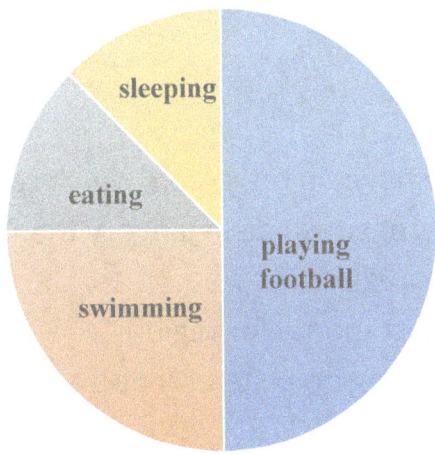

37. If Nicholas spent 2 hours sleeping, how many hours did he spend playing football?

   A. 8 hours
   B. 4 hours
   C. 6 hours
   D. 10 hours

38. A plane has a crew of 6 people and can carry a total of 20 people at any one time. How many trips will be needed to carry 80 passengers from Kingston to Montego Bay?

A. 4
B. 5
C. 6
D. 7

Look at the graph below. It shows the number of hours of sunshine per month, over a 4-month period, in 3 different regions.

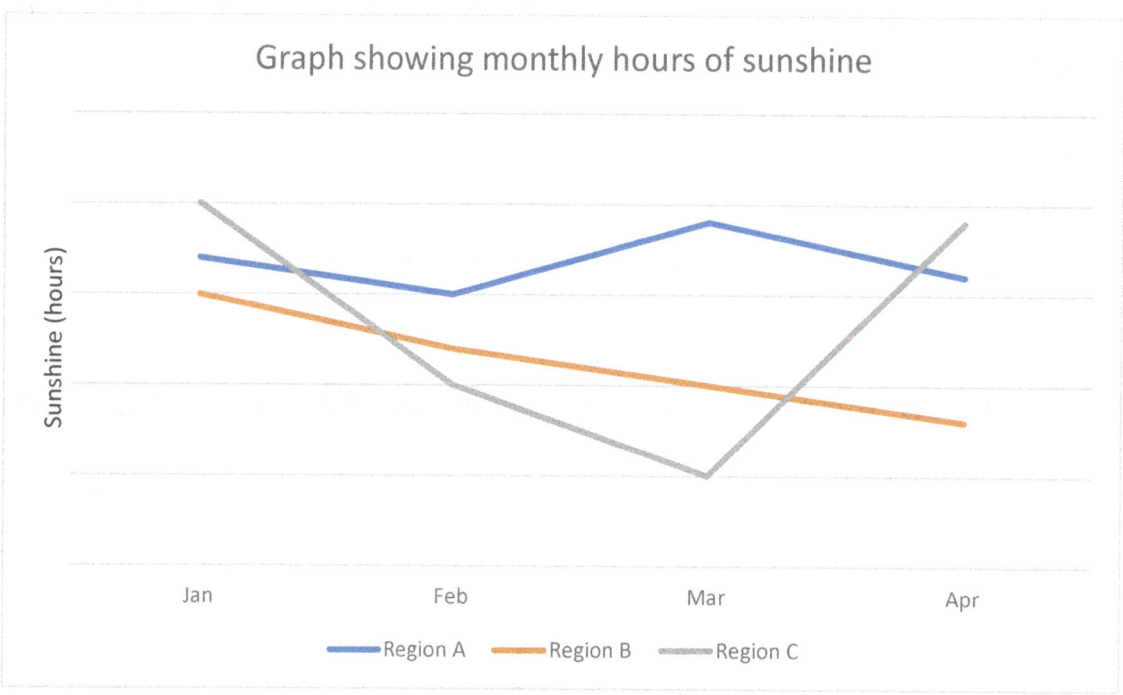

39. Based on the information shown in the graph, which conclusion is true?
A. There were fewer hours of sunshine in January than in February.
B. Region B is the sunniest region.
C. February was the sunniest month for region C.
D. The hours of sunshine in region B steadily decreased.

40. A fisherman has three types of fish in his net. There is the same number of soldier fish as there is the number of herring. Half of the fish are snappers. Which of the following numbers **could** be the total number of fish in the net?

A. 60
B. 45
C. 33
D. 54

EVALUATE YOUR WORK!

Remember to evaluate your work and ask someone to evaluate it for you. If you don't understand, then please review the key concepts as well as ask for help.

Got it!   Almost got it!   Don't understand.

My evaluation of the test: _____

What is my plan of action? What will I do next?

....
....
....
....
....
....

40-QUESTIONS TEST #2
ANSWER SHEET

The next page has an answer sheet that you will use to record your answers. It is like the one you will most likely use during your PEP exams. Please remove this page.

(OPTIONAL HELPFUL INFORMATION)

TEST #: _____

START TIME: _____

END TIME: _____

SCORE: _____

'The key to realizing a dream is to focus not on success but significance, and then even the small steps and little victories along your path will take on greater meaning.'

— OPRAH WINFREY —

Start this test whenever you are told to do so or whenever you are ready.

40-QUESTIONS TEST #2

Name: _____ ID no. _____ Age: ___

School: _____ School address: _____

#					#				
1	A	B	C	D	21	A	B	C	D
2	A	B	C	D	22	A	B	C	D
3	A	B	C	D	23	A	B	C	D
4	A	B	C	D	24	A	B	C	D
5	A	B	C	D	25	A	B	C	D
6	A	B	C	D	26	A	B	C	D
7	A	B	C	D	27	A	B	C	D
8	A	B	C	D	28	A	B	C	D
9	A	B	C	D	29	A	B	C	D
10	A	B	C	D	30	A	B	C	D
11	A	B	C	D	31	A	B	C	D
12	A	B	C	D	32	A	B	C	D
13	A	B	C	D	33	A	B	C	D
14	A	B	C	D	34	A	B	C	D
15	A	B	C	D	35	A	B	C	D
16	A	B	C	D	36	A	B	C	D
17	A	B	C	D	37	A	B	C	D
18	A	B	C	D	38	A	B	C	D
19	A	B	C	D	39	A	B	C	D
20	A	B	C	D	40	A	B	C	D

Score _____ out of 40

www.mycheetahacademy.com

40-QUESTIONS TEST #2

The diagram below represents a number. Each individual cube in the diagram has a value of 1. Use the diagram to answer the question that follows.

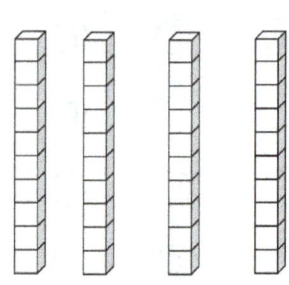
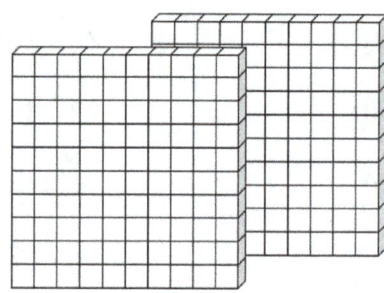
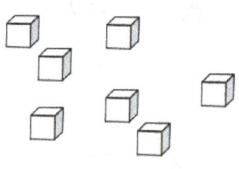

1. Which number does the diagram show?

    A. 427   B. 247   C. 2470   D. 4207

For items 2 and 3, select the word that best completes each sentence.

2. The noise that warns you of danger is an_____.

    A. arm   B. art   C. alarm   D. ant

3. A doe is a female deer. A_____ is a female lion.

    A. cat   B. tiger   C. goat   D. lioness

4. Identify what comes next in the sequence.

        cotton, yarn, fabric, _____

    A. flower   B. dress   C. bread   D. pen

5. Select the number that comes next in the sequence of the numbers below.

    1, 3, 6, 10, 15, ____, 28, 36, 45

    A. 12   B. 11   C. 55   D. 21

6. The numbers in each triangle below follow the same rule. Use the first two triangles to help you find the missing number in the third one.

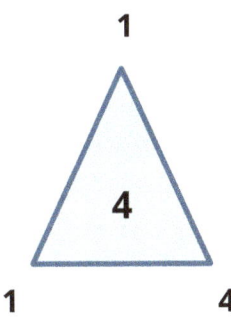

4	1	2
12	4	?
7 9	1 4	6 5

A. 4　　　　　B. 8　　　　　C. 9　　　　　D. 1

These prepositions can change the meaning of the verb 'take'. Check the following different meanings, then answer items 7 and 8.

Take in means to understand.

Take through means to explain something.

Take down means to write notes.

Take off means to run away or fly in the air.

7. We stood at the beach and watched the airplane _____.
  A. take down
  B. take through
  C. take in
  D. take off

8. Fred searched for his notebook to _____ some notes in it.
  A. take down
  B. take through
  C. take in
  D. take off

9. You have a total of 6 marbles in a bag, and they are all blue. If you select 1 without looking, how likely is it to be blue?
  A. unlikely　　　B. likely　　　C. impossible　　　D. certain

The diagram below shows a parallelogram WXYZ.

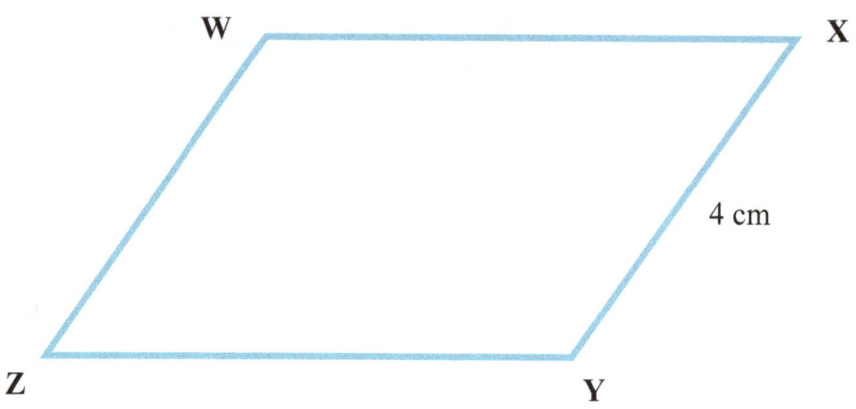

10. If the perimeter of WXYZ is 20 cm, then the base length is _____ cm.

    A. 6   B. 4   C. 8   D. 3

For items 11 to 13, select the most appropriate word or phrase to complete each sentence.

11. Dark rain clouds give out thunder and _____.

    A. lightning   B. snow   C. light   D. sunlight

12. It's hot today. You can _____ your jacket.

    A. take on   B. take off   C. take in   D. take up

13. The nutrients in our food which are responsible for building strong muscles are _____.

    A. carbohydrates   B. vitamins   C. fats   D. proteins

14. Michael kicked a ball 13 m. Charles kicked a ball 3 times as far. How far did Charles' ball go?

    A. 36 m   B. 39 m   C. 22 m   D. 33 m

The pictures below show the life cycle of a butterfly. Use them to answer item 15.

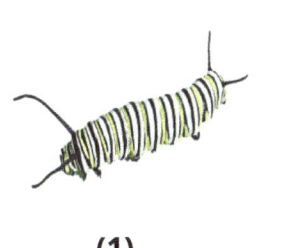   

(1)   (2)   (3)   (4)

15. Which of the following options gives the logical sequence of the life cycle of the butterfly?

A. 4, 1, 2, 3   B. 2, 4, 3, 1   C. 1, 4, 3, 2   D. 2, 3, 4, 1

16. Mark has 6 dollars. He wants to buy hot dogs. The price of 1 hot dog is 2 dollars. What is the maximum number of hotdogs he can buy?

A. 6   B. 2   C. 4   D. 3

For items 17 and 18, select the word that is a necessary component of the underlined word.

17. <u>computer</u>

A. pencil   B. keyboard   C. pen   D. book

18. <u>classroom</u>

A. net   B. bed   C. board   D. ball

19. There are about 310 passengers in each car of the city train. If there are 8 cars on the train, about how many passengers are on the train?

A. 240   B. 2,004   C. 2,400   D. 2,500

Examine the 3 shapes and answer item 20.

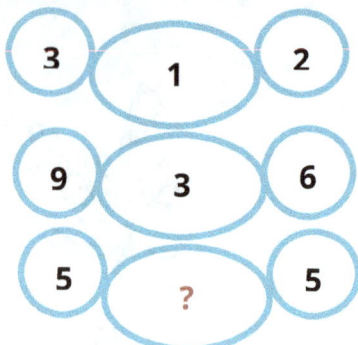

20. Which number should replace the question mark?

A. 0 B. 5 C. 22 D. 3

Anne is thinking of a number. She gives the following clues:

The first digit is half of the number 10.
The second digit is 3 less than 7.
The number is odd.

21. What number is Anne thinking of?

A. 526 B. 444 C. 545 D. 459

22. Kelly is practising for a math competition. She should be able to calculate about 18 problems within 180 minutes. About how much time will she have for each problem?

A. 6 minutes B. 10 minutes C. 100 minutes D. 16 minutes

23. Use the table below to find the next pair of letters in the series.

A	B	C	D	E	F	G	H	I	J	K	L	M	N	O	P	Q	R	S	T
1	2	3	4	5	6	7	8	9	10	11	12	13	14	15	16	17	18	19	20

AN   CM   EL   ____

A. FL
B. JH
C. GK
D. HJ

For items 24 and 25, select the word that DOES NOT belong to the group.

24. A. Saturday   B. Friday   C. Wednesday   D. April

25. A. water   B. ice   C. steam   D. wood

26. Which arrow points to the fraction $\frac{6}{8}$ on the number line?

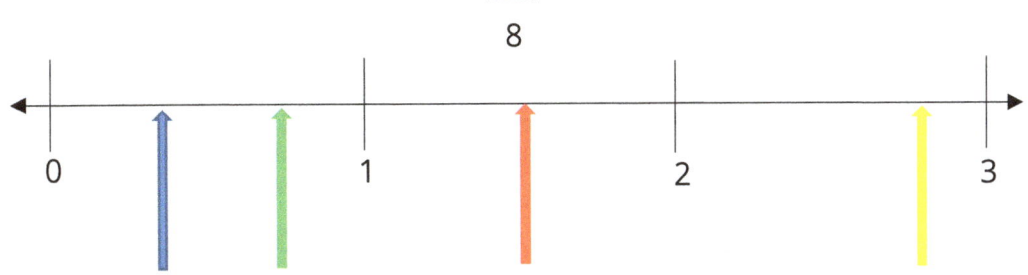

A. the blue arrow   C. the red arrow
B. the green arrow   D. the yellow arrow

A restaurant serves 3 different dishes. The table below shows the number of dishes that were served and the amount of money that was made. Use the table information to answer questions 27 and 28.

Dishes	Week 1		Week 2		Week 3	
	Quantity of dishes	Price ($)	Quantity of dishes	Price ($)	Quantity of dishes	Price ($)
Ackee and saltfish	15	600	10	400	10	400
Jerked chicken	10	500	17	850	20	1000
Stewed peas	7	450	30	1950	45	2925

27. In which week did the restaurant have the lowest sale(s) of jerked chicken?
A. week 1   C. week 3
B. week 2   D. weeks 2 and 3

40-QUESTIONS TEST #2

28. At the end of the 3 weeks, which dish was most popular?
 A. ackee and saltfish
 B. jerked chicken
 C. stewed peas
 D. none of the above

Read both passages then indicate whether each conclusion drawn can best be described as 'true', 'false', or 'cannot tell', in items 29 and 30.

> Pets are part of many children's lives. Big or small, furry or scaly we all love pets.
>
> They are domestic. We love to groom and feed them. They are friendly and cute.
>
> Common pets are dogs, cats, rabbits, fish and parrots.

> Wild animals live in the jungle and they often hunt to eat. They don't depend on humans.
>
> Wild animals can hurt or eat humans, so we should stay away from them.
>
> Some wild animals include lions, tigers and gorillas.

29. Wild animals are domestic.
 A. true   B. false   C. partially true   D. cannot tell

30. It is not safe to be near to a rabbit.
 A. true   B. false   C. partially true   D. cannot tell

31. Examine the words in the bubble closely, then place them in a logical sequence.

 A. teenager, baby, elder, child, adult
 B. child, elder, baby, teenager, adult
 C. elder, teenager, adult, baby, child
 D. baby, child, teenager, adult, elder

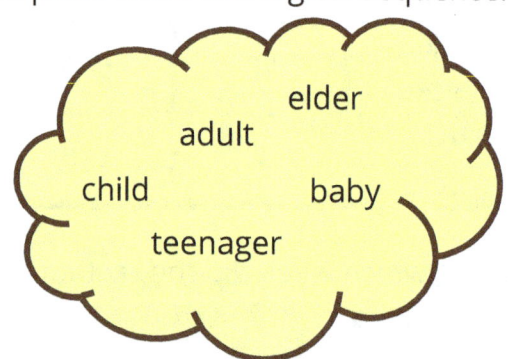

32. How many eggs would you have if you bought half a dozen?

  A. 6   B. 4   C. 3   D. 2

Examine the shapes in the boxes below, then answer the question that follows.

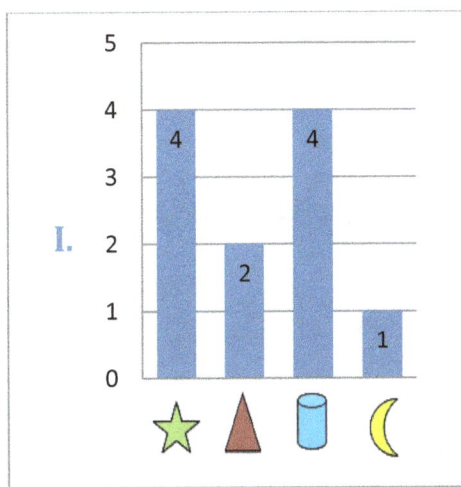
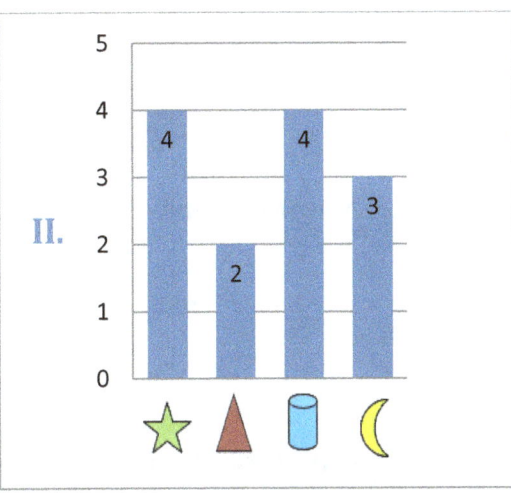
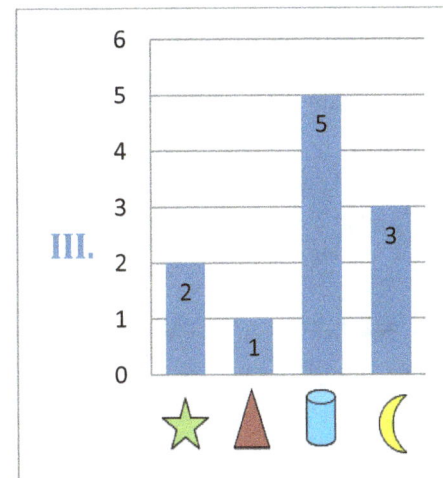
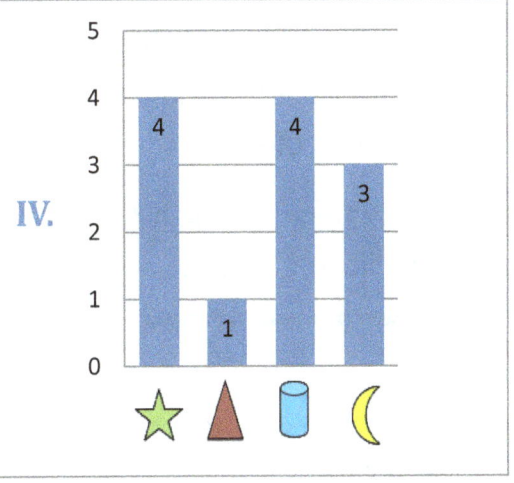

33. Which chart represents the information correctly?

  A. chart I   B. chart II   C. chart III   D. chart IV

34. A girl introduced a boy as the son of the daughter of the father of her uncle. The boy could be the girl's _____.

A. aunt
B. mother
C. son
D. brother

The diagram below shows the number of people who own various pets. Use it to answer the question that follows.

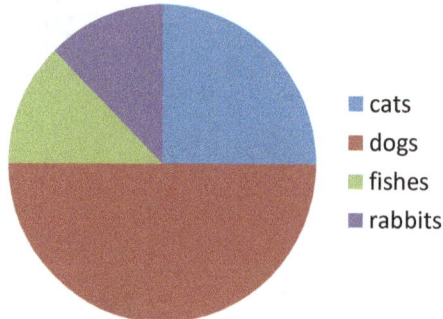

35. If there are 500 people who have dogs, about how many people have rabbits in their homes?

A. 50
B. 1000
C. 125
D. 500

Read the passage carefully, then answer items 36 and 37.

Jamaica is a mountainous island in the Caribbean Sea about 965 kilometres south of Miami, Florida. It is a part of the chain of Caribbean islands called the Greater Antilles. Jamaica is the tip of a mountain rising from the sea floor.

Jamaica was formed when the North American and the Caribbean tectonic plates collided about 25 million years ago.

36. What do you think this article is about?

A. Jamaican geography
B. Jamaican culture
C. The Jamaican flag
D. Jamaican income

37. The tip of a mountain means the _____ of it.

A. mid
B. top
C. bottom
D. middle

Examine the following shapes and answer the question that follows.

    1.   2.   3.   4.

38. Which of them are not polygons?
    A. 4, 2   B. 3, 1   C. 3, 2   D. 4, 1

Look at the wheel. It has 6 equal sections. Use the wheel to find the probability.

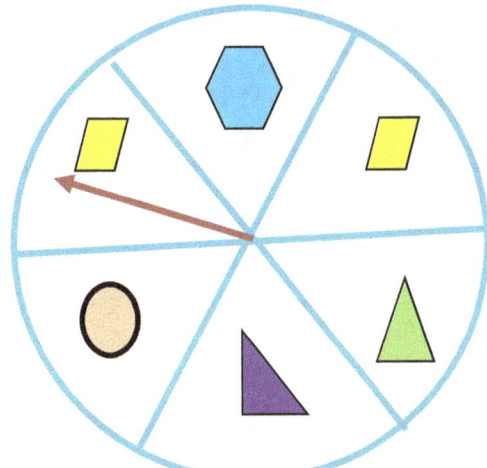

39. If you spin the wheel, what is the probability that you will land on a parallelogram?
    A. 1/3   B. 2   C. ½   D. 3

40. If you spin the wheel 60 times, how many times would you expect it to land on a triangle?
    A. 10   B. 20   C. 5   D. 60

My evaluation of the test:_____

What is my plan of action? What will I do next?

....
....
....
....
....
....

www.mycheetahacademy.com

CHEETAH™ Toys & More, LLC Copyright 2022 © Copying is NOT allowed

CHEETAH™
Connect to Higher Education, Electronic Tools, Aplication and Help

40-QUESTIONS TEST #2

Let me help you to build your knowledge, endurance and stamina for the real test. Let's go! Let's go.

Let's prep for PEP.

40-QUESTIONS TEST #3

ANSWER SHEET

The next page has an answer sheet that you will use to record your answers. It is similar to the one you will most likely use during your PEP exams. Please remove this page.

(OPTIONAL HELPFUL INFORMATION)

TEST #: _____

START TIME: _____

END TIME: _____

SCORE: _____

'You may not control all the events that happen to you, but you can decide not to be reduced by them.'

– MAYA ANGELOU –

Start this test whenever you are told to do so or whenever you are ready.

40-QUESTIONS TEST #3

Name: _____   ID no. _____   Age: ___

School: _____   School address: _____

1	Ⓐ	Ⓑ	Ⓒ	Ⓓ	21	Ⓐ	Ⓑ	Ⓒ	Ⓓ
2	Ⓐ	Ⓑ	Ⓒ	Ⓓ	22	Ⓐ	Ⓑ	Ⓒ	Ⓓ
3	Ⓐ	Ⓑ	Ⓒ	Ⓓ	23	Ⓐ	Ⓑ	Ⓒ	Ⓓ
4	Ⓐ	Ⓑ	Ⓒ	Ⓓ	24	Ⓐ	Ⓑ	Ⓒ	Ⓓ
5	Ⓐ	Ⓑ	Ⓒ	Ⓓ	25	Ⓐ	Ⓑ	Ⓒ	Ⓓ
6	Ⓐ	Ⓑ	Ⓒ	Ⓓ	26	Ⓐ	Ⓑ	Ⓒ	Ⓓ
7	Ⓐ	Ⓑ	Ⓒ	Ⓓ	27	Ⓐ	Ⓑ	Ⓒ	Ⓓ
8	Ⓐ	Ⓑ	Ⓒ	Ⓓ	28	Ⓐ	Ⓑ	Ⓒ	Ⓓ
9	Ⓐ	Ⓑ	Ⓒ	Ⓓ	29	Ⓐ	Ⓑ	Ⓒ	Ⓓ
10	Ⓐ	Ⓑ	Ⓒ	Ⓓ	30	Ⓐ	Ⓑ	Ⓒ	Ⓓ
11	Ⓐ	Ⓑ	Ⓒ	Ⓓ	31	Ⓐ	Ⓑ	Ⓒ	Ⓓ
12	Ⓐ	Ⓑ	Ⓒ	Ⓓ	32	Ⓐ	Ⓑ	Ⓒ	Ⓓ
13	Ⓐ	Ⓑ	Ⓒ	Ⓓ	33	Ⓐ	Ⓑ	Ⓒ	Ⓓ
14	Ⓐ	Ⓑ	Ⓒ	Ⓓ	34	Ⓐ	Ⓑ	Ⓒ	Ⓓ
15	Ⓐ	Ⓑ	Ⓒ	Ⓓ	35	Ⓐ	Ⓑ	Ⓒ	Ⓓ
16	Ⓐ	Ⓑ	Ⓒ	Ⓓ	36	Ⓐ	Ⓑ	Ⓒ	Ⓓ
17	Ⓐ	Ⓑ	Ⓒ	Ⓓ	37	Ⓐ	Ⓑ	Ⓒ	Ⓓ
18	Ⓐ	Ⓑ	Ⓒ	Ⓓ	38	Ⓐ	Ⓑ	Ⓒ	Ⓓ
19	Ⓐ	Ⓑ	Ⓒ	Ⓓ	39	Ⓐ	Ⓑ	Ⓒ	Ⓓ
20	Ⓐ	Ⓑ	Ⓒ	Ⓓ	40	Ⓐ	Ⓑ	Ⓒ	Ⓓ

Score _____ **out of 40**

40-QUESTIONS TEST #3

For items 1 to 4, select the word that DOES NOT belong to the group.

1. A. passport   B. bird   C. airport   D. luggage

2. A. fish   B. snake   C. crocodile   D. whale

3. A. copper   B. iron   C. iodine   D. tin

4. A. cuboid   B. triangle   C. rectangle   D. square

Examine the shapes and complete item 5.

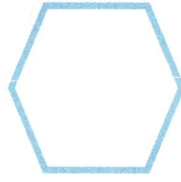
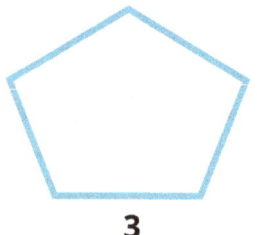

1   2   3   4

5. The hexagon is shape number _____.

   A. 1   B. 2   C. 3   D. 4

Read the following paragraph carefully and complete item 6.

Sweets and chocolates and Chips is fun to eat sometimes but it is not good to eat them every day. These foods contain too much sugar, fat or salt. Fruit and vegetables helps you stay health and grow strong.

6. There are _____ errors in the paragraph.

   A. 4   B. 5   C. 6   D. 0

Examine the 3 shapes below and answer item 7.

7. Which number should replace the question mark?

A. 88
B. 81
C. 28
D. 18

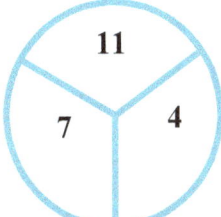
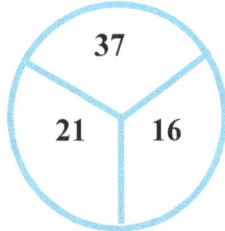
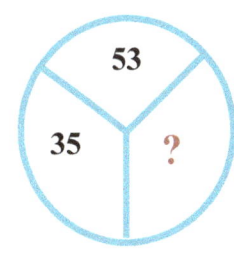

For items 8 to 12, select the correct answer.

8. I heard the car's_____ and got ready to leave.
  A. cry B. laugh C. scream D. horn

9. Forest is to tree as tree is to _____ .
  A. plant B. leaf C. soil D. Earth

10. To get to school each day, Ms Dana takes a JUTC bus and a taxi. If the bus takes 23 minutes and the taxi takes 49 minutes, what is her daily travelling time from home to school?
  A. 1 hour and 2 minutes
  B. 1 hour and 12 minutes
  C. 73 minutes
  D. 82 minutes

11. Brad has 6 more fish than Michael. Together, they have 18 fish. How many fish does Brad have?
  A. 6 B. 10 C. 8 D. 12

12. There can be a right angle and an obtuse angle in one triangle.
  A. agree
  B. disagree
  C. cannot tell
  D. have to use a protractor

Examine ABC right-angled triangle, then answer item 13. Remember that all the angles of a triangle add up to 180 degrees. Find the unknown angle.

13. The angle of BAC equals _____ º.
  A. 130
  B. 40
  C. 50
  D. 90

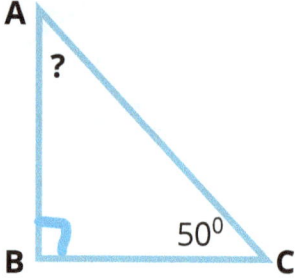

Read both passages carefully, then complete items 14 and 15.

Channel 4

Don't miss tonight's big game! Jamaica will play Curacao for a place in this year's Caribbean Cup final! Kick off is at 6:30 pm at the Olympic Stadium in Martinique. Both teams are very strong. Join us live to find out which team is going to the final.

Channel 3

The Galapagos Islands are home to unusual plants and animals, such as giant tortoises and colourful crabs. How did wildlife come to this group of islands? Find out as we explore the islands.

14. You can learn about animals on Channel 3.
  A. true
  B. false
  C. partially true
  D. unable to tell

15. Channels 3 and 4 are _____ channels respectively.
  A. entertainment and sports
  B. educational and documentary
  C. sports and documentary
  D. sports and movie

40-QUESTIONS TEST #3

16. From the sum of 8 and 9, take their difference.

   A. 72   B. 1   C. 17   D. 16

For items 17 to 20, select the most appropriate word to complete each sentence.

17. Hard is to difficult, as simple is to _____.
- A. good
- B. awful
- C. easy
- D. challenging

18. It is believed that the Coronavirus could have originated in _____.
- A. chicken
- B. monkeys
- C. dogs
- D. rat bats

19. A baby cat is called a kitten. A baby cow is called a_____.
- A. lamb
- B. calf
- C. kitten
- D. puppy

20. When we travel, we put our things in bags called_____.
- A. luggage
- B. pouch
- C. wallet
- D. briefcase

21. Select the letters that come next in the sequence shown below.
   Sequence: AZ, BY, CX, ?

   A. PQ   B. RS   C. DW   D. EV

40-QUESTIONS TEST #3

The following double-bars graph shows the marks of 4 pupils in math and science. Examine it well, then answer items 22 and 23.

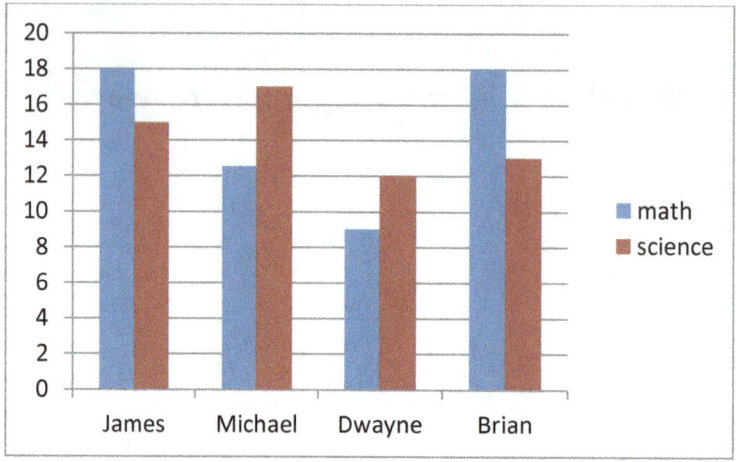

22. Which pupil got the highest marks in math and science combined?

    A. James   C. Dwayne

    B. Michael   D. Brian

23. Which pupil got the lowest mark in math?

    A. James   C. Dwayne

    B. Michael   D. Brian

Read the following definitions carefully and identify the objects by selecting the correct option in items 24 to 26.

24. A _____ is an instrument used to look at the stars.

    A. teleport   C. microscope

    B. telescope   C. telephone

25. A_____ is a very brief period.

    A. hour   C. moment

    B. monument   D. none of the above

26. A _____ is a young horse.

    A. horse   C. foal

    B. piglet   D. lamb

A survey of our factory's weekly production was done. The following information was gathered:
- ✓ The factory produced 60 TVs.
- ✓ It produced fewer fridges than heaters.
- ✓ It produced 40 fans.

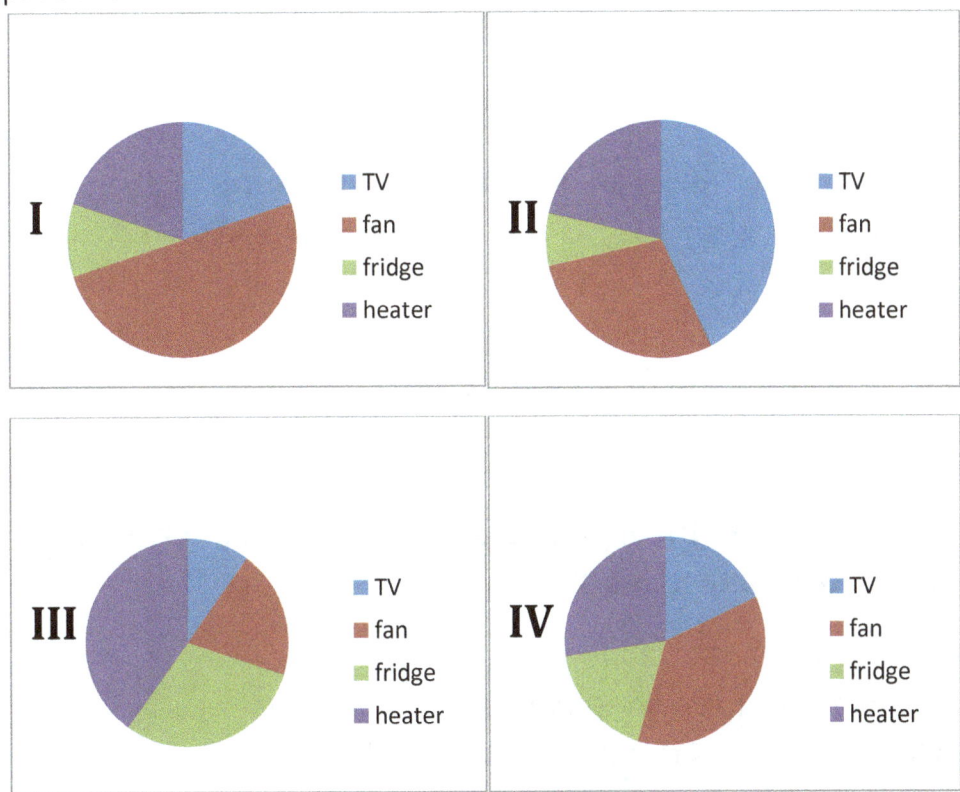

27. Which chart represents the correct information?

   A. chart I   B. chart II   C. chart III   D. chart IV

Read the passage carefully, then complete items 28 and 29.

Shadow puppet theatres first started in China thousands of years ago, but <u>they</u> are still popular today in many parts of the world. Shadow puppets tell people about important events and describe traditional stories. Nowadays, there are some modern stories too. Often, there is just one puppeteer who makes the puppet move by using a stick on its back.

28. The theatre shows are always about old stories.

   A. true   B. false   C. unable to tell   D. partially true

40-QUESTIONS TEST #3

29. The pronoun *they* in the first line refers to_____.
    A. the puppets   C. shadow puppet theatres
    B. China   D. can't tell

30. Your father stops for fuel and finds that it costs $139 per litre. His total fuel bill is $1,390. How many litres of fuel did he buy?
    A. 50 litres   B. 20 litres   C. 10 litres   D. 30 litres

31. Which weighs more, 1 kilogram of stones or 1 kilogram of feathers?
    A. 1 kilogram of stones   C. both are equal
    B. 1 kilogram of feathers   D. impossible to tell

32. Add the sum of 6 and 5 to their product.
    A. 30   B. 41   C. 11   D. 65

Prepositions can change the meaning of the verb *break*. Check the following meanings, then complete items 33 and 34.

    Break down means to stop working.
    Break up means to end or separate.
    Break in/into means to enter a place illegally.
    Break out means to escape from a place.

33. The car _____ so, they travelled by train.
    A. broke into   C. broke down
    B. broke into   D. broke up

34. When the thieves _____ the bank, the security alarm sounded.
    A. broke into   C. broke down
    B. broke in   D. broke up

35. Your aunt wants to make a rectangular-shaped picture frame for a rectangular-shaped picture which measures 140 cm by 60 cm. If the cost of one metre of the frame is $5, what is the cost of the frame?
    A. $5   B. $10   C. $100   D. $20

36. Kimberly tosses 2 coins. Each coin has 2 possible outcomes: H (heads) and T (tails). Find the probability that Kimberly tosses 2 heads.

    A. 2 / 3   C. 6 / 4

    B. 2 / 4   D. 1 / 4

37. A card is drawn from a pack of 52 cards. The probability of getting a queen of clubs or king of hearts is _____.

    A. 1 / 26   C. 1 / 52

    B. 3 / 26   D. 3 / 52

The pictures below show how chocolate is made. Use them to answer item 38.

(1)   (2)

(3)   (4)

38. Which one of the following gives the logical steps to making chocolate?

    A. 1, 2, 3, 4   C. 1, 4, 3, 2

    B. 4, 1, 3, 2   D. 4, 3, 2, 1

The diagram below shows the number of people who tested positive for the Coronavirus during a single month. Examine it carefully and answer items 39 and 40.

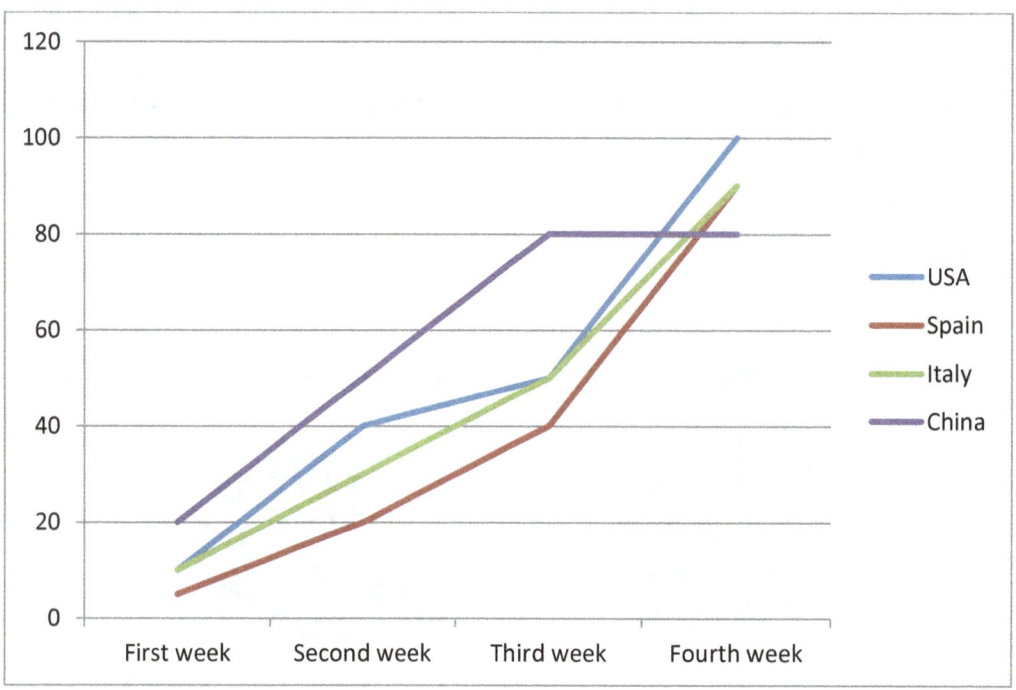

39. Which country had no increase in cases in the last two weeks?

    A. USA   C. Italy

    B. Spain   D. China

40. Which country had the greatest number of cases during the fourth week?

    A. USA   C. Italy

    B. Spain   D. China

EVALUATE YOUR WORK!

Remember to evaluate your work and ask someone to evaluate it for you. If you don't understand, then please review the key concepts as well as ask for help.

- 😊 Got it!
- 😐 Almost got it!
- ☹️ Don't understand.

My evaluation of the test:_____

What is my plan of action? What will I do next?

....
....
....
....
....
....

40-QUESTIONS TEST #4

ANSWER SHEET

The next page has an answer sheet that you will use to record your answers. It is similar to the one you will most likely use during your PEP exams. Please remove this page.

(OPTIONAL HELPFUL INFORMATION)

TEST #: _____

START TIME: _____

END TIME: _____

SCORE: _____

'The heights by great men reached and kept were not attained by sudden flight, but they, while their companions slept, were toiling upward in the night.'

– HENRY LONGFELLOW –

Start this test whenever you are told to do so or whenever you are ready.

40-QUESTIONS TEST #4

Name: _____ ID no. _____ Age: ___

School: _____ School address: _____

1	Ⓐ	Ⓑ	Ⓒ	Ⓓ	21	Ⓐ	Ⓑ	Ⓒ	Ⓓ
2	Ⓐ	Ⓑ	Ⓒ	Ⓓ	22	Ⓐ	Ⓑ	Ⓒ	Ⓓ
3	Ⓐ	Ⓑ	Ⓒ	Ⓓ	23	Ⓐ	Ⓑ	Ⓒ	Ⓓ
4	Ⓐ	Ⓑ	Ⓒ	Ⓓ	24	Ⓐ	Ⓑ	Ⓒ	Ⓓ
5	Ⓐ	Ⓑ	Ⓒ	Ⓓ	25	Ⓐ	Ⓑ	Ⓒ	Ⓓ
6	Ⓐ	Ⓑ	Ⓒ	Ⓓ	26	Ⓐ	Ⓑ	Ⓒ	Ⓓ
7	Ⓐ	Ⓑ	Ⓒ	Ⓓ	27	Ⓐ	Ⓑ	Ⓒ	Ⓓ
8	Ⓐ	Ⓑ	Ⓒ	Ⓓ	28	Ⓐ	Ⓑ	Ⓒ	Ⓓ
9	Ⓐ	Ⓑ	Ⓒ	Ⓓ	29	Ⓐ	Ⓑ	Ⓒ	Ⓓ
10	Ⓐ	Ⓑ	Ⓒ	Ⓓ	30	Ⓐ	Ⓑ	Ⓒ	Ⓓ
11	Ⓐ	Ⓑ	Ⓒ	Ⓓ	31	Ⓐ	Ⓑ	Ⓒ	Ⓓ
12	Ⓐ	Ⓑ	Ⓒ	Ⓓ	32	Ⓐ	Ⓑ	Ⓒ	Ⓓ
13	Ⓐ	Ⓑ	Ⓒ	Ⓓ	33	Ⓐ	Ⓑ	Ⓒ	Ⓓ
14	Ⓐ	Ⓑ	Ⓒ	Ⓓ	34	Ⓐ	Ⓑ	Ⓒ	Ⓓ
15	Ⓐ	Ⓑ	Ⓒ	Ⓓ	35	Ⓐ	Ⓑ	Ⓒ	Ⓓ
16	Ⓐ	Ⓑ	Ⓒ	Ⓓ	36	Ⓐ	Ⓑ	Ⓒ	Ⓓ
17	Ⓐ	Ⓑ	Ⓒ	Ⓓ	37	Ⓐ	Ⓑ	Ⓒ	Ⓓ
18	Ⓐ	Ⓑ	Ⓒ	Ⓓ	38	Ⓐ	Ⓑ	Ⓒ	Ⓓ
19	Ⓐ	Ⓑ	Ⓒ	Ⓓ	39	Ⓐ	Ⓑ	Ⓒ	Ⓓ
20	Ⓐ	Ⓑ	Ⓒ	Ⓓ	40	Ⓐ	Ⓑ	Ⓒ	Ⓓ

Score _____ **out of 40**

40-QUESTIONS TEST #4

For items 1 to 3, choose the best word to complete each statement.

1. A shepherd _____ to his flocks
   A. rends   B. stands   C. tends   D. hands

2. The bird _____ high above the rooftops.
   A. flew   B. flu   C. flue   D. flow

3. The boy _____ with his brother over whose turn it is to do the chores.
   A. altercations   B. tiffs   C. disputes   D. squabbles

4. Antony estimated that there were 40,000 people at the football match. Of the following numbers, which could **not** be the actual number of people at the match when rounded off to the nearest thousand?
   A. 39,567   B. 40,571   C. 39,985   D. 40,475

The table below shows how different age groups in a small town spend their leisure time. The information focuses on socialising, exercising and entertainment viewing, and how much time is spent on each activity.

Activity	Hours of leisure time per year			
	Teens	20–39 year olds	40–59 year olds	60+ year olds
Watching TV/DVDs	400	600	600	900
Streaming	1,200	700	150	50
Going to the cinema	100	200	100	50
Socialising with 3 or fewer people	150	300	200	200
Socialising with 4 or more people	400	350	100	50
Exercising alone	100	300	200	200
Exercising in a group/ playing sport	600	200	50	0

www.mycheetahacademy.com

40-QUESTIONS TEST #4

Use the information in the table to answer items 5 and 6.

5. Which age group spends the most time socialising with 3 or fewer people?
   - A. teens
   - B. 20 to 39-year-olds
   - C. 40 to 59-year-olds
   - D. 60+ year-olds

6. How many **more** hours per year do adults 60 years and older spend exercising alone when compared to teens?
   - A. 50 hours
   - B. 75 hours
   - C. 100 hours
   - D. 125 hours

7. Jada is half as tall as Ajani. Kevin is 5 cm shorter than Ajani, and Adam is the tallest. Which is the correct order of the children by height, from shortest to tallest?
   - A. Jada, Kevin, Adam, Ajani
   - B. Kevin, Jada, Ajani, Adam
   - C. Jada, Kevin, Ajani, Adam
   - D. Adam, Ajani, Kevin, Jada

8. Choose the right option to complete the sequence.
   egg, caterpillar, chrysalis, _____
   - A. wings
   - B. butterfly
   - C. fly
   - D. antennae

For items 9 and 10, choose the word that is an essential part of the underlined word.

9. sieve
   - A. metal
   - B. handle
   - C. holes
   - D. plastic

10. aeroplane
    - A. wings
    - B. seats
    - C. pilot
    - D. windows

40-QUESTIONS TEST #4

Below are two boxes, each containing an extract. Read the texts, then decide whether the conclusions reached in items 11 and 12 are 'true, false, partically true or unable to tell.'

Extract 1

Auckland is the largest city in New Zealand, located on the North Island. It lies on and around a narrow piece of land connecting the Northland Peninsula to the rest of New Zealand's North Island.

In 1950, Auckland hosted its first Commonwealth Games, where Malaysia and Nigeria made their first appearance.

Extract 2

Kingston is the largest city of Jamaica, and it is the capital. It is situated on the south-eastern coast of the island, on a natural harbour protected by a long sand spit.

In 1966, Kingston hosted the Commonwealth Games. For the first time since 1950, the event programme was altered to include badminton and shooting instead of rowing and lawn bowls.

11. The Auckland is located on the North Island of which country?
    A. Kingston
    B. Nigeria
    C. New Zealand
    D. Malaysia

12. In what year did Jamaica host the first Commonwealth Games?
    A. 1950
    B. 1966
    C. 1962
    D. 1998

13. John and Mary decided to share the cost of a bulla cake which costs $80.00. John gave her $20. What fraction of the cake should he get?
    A. 1/4
    B. 1/2
    C. 3/8
    D. 3/4

14. To the product of 6 and 8, add their sum.
    A. 48
    B. 34
    C. 62
    D. 68

Read the passage below before answering items 15, 16 and 17.

There are few people in the world who have not heard of Usain Bolt, widely regarded as the greatest sprinter of all time. Born in Montego Bay, Jamaica, Bolt had won gold in the 200 m by age 15, making him the youngest-ever male world junior champion in any event. He has gone on to become the only <u>athlete</u> to win gold medals for the 100 m and 200 m sprints at three Olympic Games <u>in a row</u>.

Interestingly, as a child, Bolt was drawn towards the sports of cricket and football before being steered towards athletics by his school coaches. He was a big fan of Real Madrid and Manchester United, and after retiring from the track, he tried to pursue a career in professional football. However, after spending time on trial with several clubs, Bolt is now focussing on being a businessman.

15. _____ means the same as 'in a row'.
    A. well-attended
    B. important
    C. European
    D. consecutive

16. Which of these people would also be considered an athlete?
    A. a chef
    B. a tennis player
    C. a writer
    D. a musician

17. What is the writer most surprised about?
    A. Usain Bolt was drawn towards cricket and football before athletics.
    B. Usain Bolt won so many gold medals.
    C. There are few people in the world who have not heard of Usain Bolt.
    D. Usain Bolt is now focussing on being a businessman.

40-QUESTIONS TEST #4

For items 18 to 20 below, choose the word that DOES NOT fit the group.

18. A. mother
    B. father
    C. uncle
    D. brother-in-law

19. A. sandals
    B. slippers
    C. socks
    D. sneakers

20. A. terminate
    B. end
    C. finish
    D. discard

21. Look closely at the words in the box, then choose the logical sequence from small to big.

    Kingston   world   universe   Jamaica

    A. Jamaica, Kingston, universe, world
    B. Kingston, Jamaica, world, universe
    C. world, universe, Jamaica, Kingston
    D. universe, world, Kingston, Jamaica

22. Choose the numbers that complete the following sequence:
    2, 3, 5, 7, 11, 13, ___, ___
    A. 15, 16
    B. 17, 20
    C. 23, 25
    D. 17, 23

Look at the graph below. It shows the change in the number of people visiting Jamaica between 2005 and 2019.

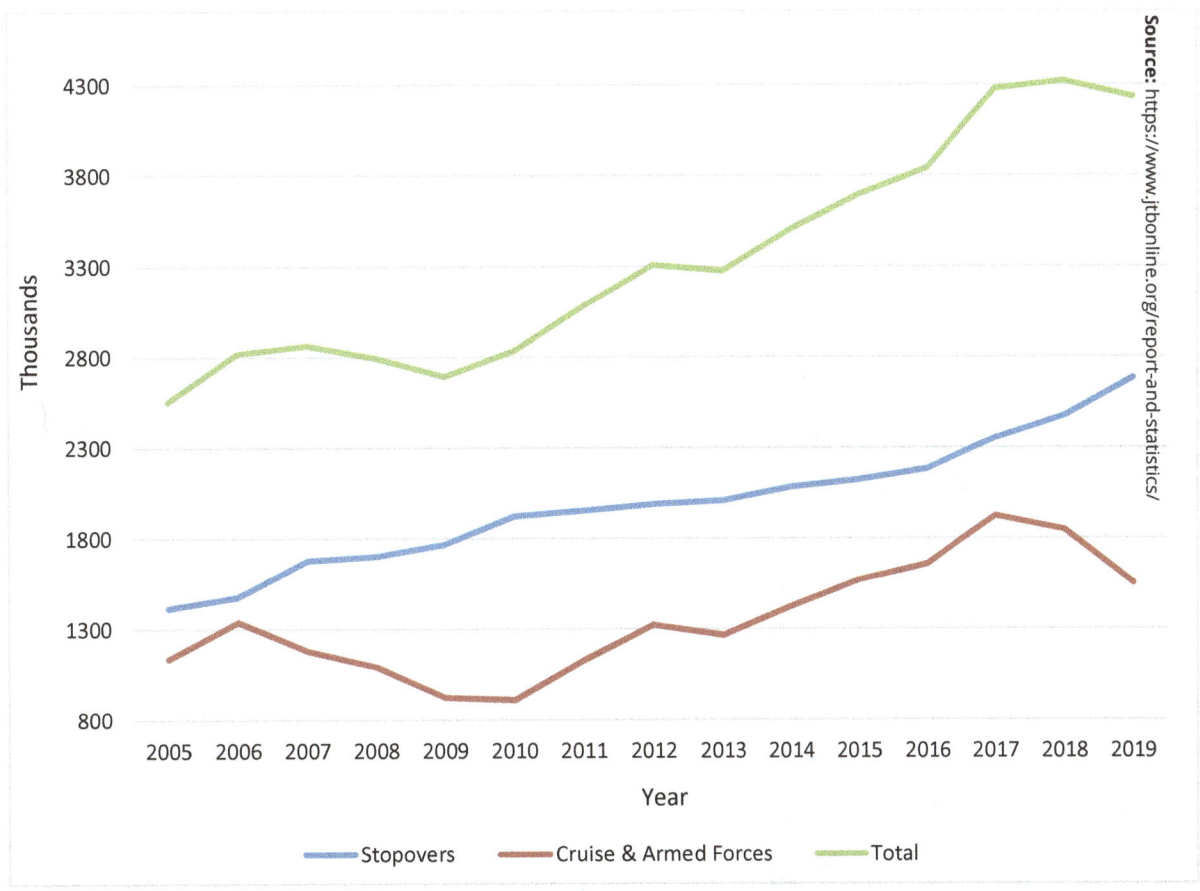

23. Based on the information shown in the graph, which conclusion is true?
    A. More people visited in 2009 than in 2008.
    B. Fewer people visited for stopovers than cruises and armed forces visits.
    C. The greatest number of visitors came to Jamaica in 2018.
    D. The number of people visiting with cruises or armed forces has steadily increased.

24. Divide the sum of 15 and 20 by the difference between them.
    A. 14
    B. 35
    C. 7
    D. 26

25. Using the numbers 3, 4. 5, 6 and 7, complete the grid so that the sum of all numbers in each row and column equals 15.

4	5	T
R	5	3
4	P	6

A. R =3, P =5 and T= 3
B. R =7, P =5 and T= 6
C. R =4, P =5 and T= 4
D. R =3, P =5 and T= 6

26. Toby is heading home from school when his teacher asks him to buy some tinned pineapple from the market for the school fair. Toby has a backpack and can carry a total of 10 tins at any one time, but he already has 4 tins of tomatoes packed for his mother. How many trips will be needed to carry 20 tins of pineapple to the teacher before Toby can head home to his mother with her tomatoes?

A. 2   B. 3   C. 4   D. 5

27. If it takes 50 kilograms to break a spring, how many 2-kilogram weights would be needed to break the spring?

A. 10   B. 30   C. 100   D. 25

28. Sam wants to add marbles to a plastic toy boat until it sinks in her swimming pool. What information does she need to work out how many marbles she must have?

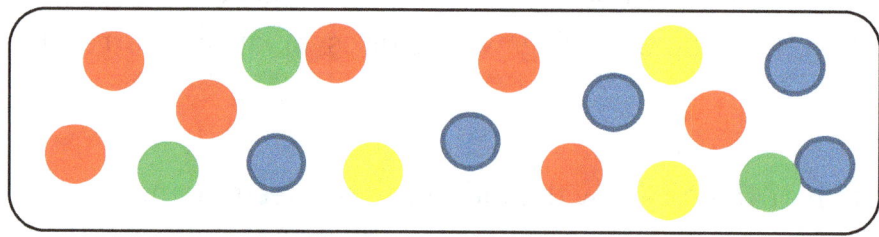

A. The weight required to sink the plastic toy boat.
B. The capacity of the plastic toy boat.
C. The circumference of each marble.
D. The number of marbles she has.

Look at the diagram below. It shows the colours of the proportions of 4 types of sweets in a bag. Half of the sweets are red and a quarter of them are yellow. Of the remainder, half are green and half purple.

29. Which of the following COULD be the number of sweets in the bag?

  A. 54 B. 48 C. 50 D. 38

Below is a diagram of a square (ABCD) joined to a rectangle (DEFG).

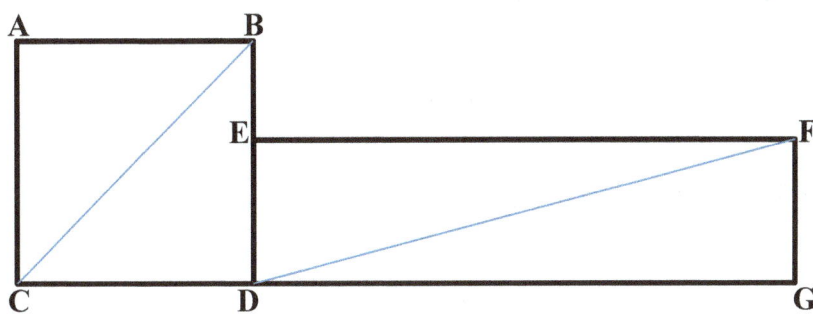

30. The greatest length is shown by which of the following?

  A. AC + DG
  B. BE + DF
  C. DG + EF
  D. CG + DF

40-QUESTIONS TEST #4

31. If ▦ shows ◗ then ▦ shows _____.

A. ◿

B. ◔

C. ◔

D. ◕

For the items 32 to 35, choose the word that best finishes each sentence.

32. Snow is to winter as sunshine is to _____.
    A. summer   C. light
    B. warmth   D. day

33. Butterfly is to caterpillar as _____ is to tadpole.
    A. lizard   C. dragonfly
    B. frog   D. fish

34. Wide is to narrow as early is to _____.
    A. time   C. morning
    B. quick   D. late

35. Stop is to go as _____ is to rough.
    A. smooth   C. kind
    B. bumpy   D. texture

36. Jasmine is reading an alphabet book to her younger brother. She notices that the letter 'A' appears on a right-hand page. When she turns the page over, the letter 'B' is on the left-hand side and faces the letter 'C' on the right. Which of the following pairs of letters will also face each other?
    A. I and J   C. Q and R
    B. N and O   D. U and V

The steps for making a burger are shown in the pictures below.

1.

2.

3.

4.

5.

37. Which of the following sequences puts the steps for making a burger in logical order?

A. 4, 5, 3, 1, 2

B. 3, 1, 4, 5, 2

C. 3, 5, 1, 4, 2

D. 1, 4, 5, 2, 3

In a survey, 80 Grade 6 students were asked about their favourite way to spend their spare time.

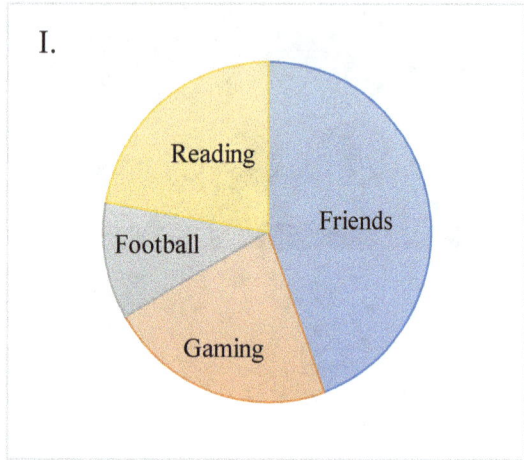

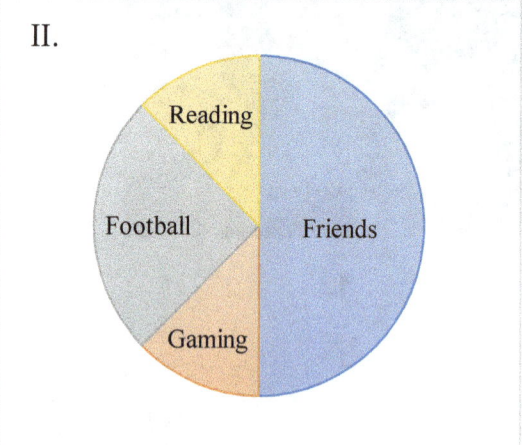

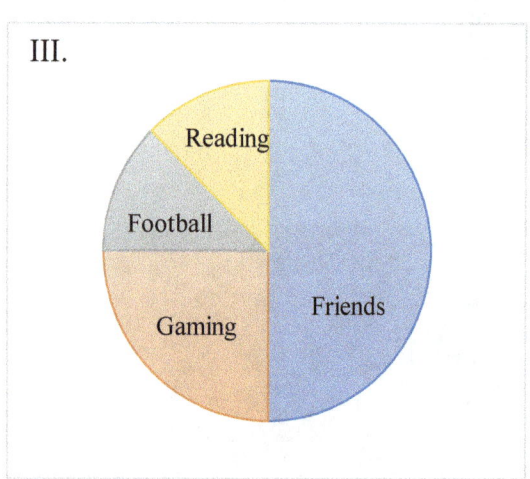

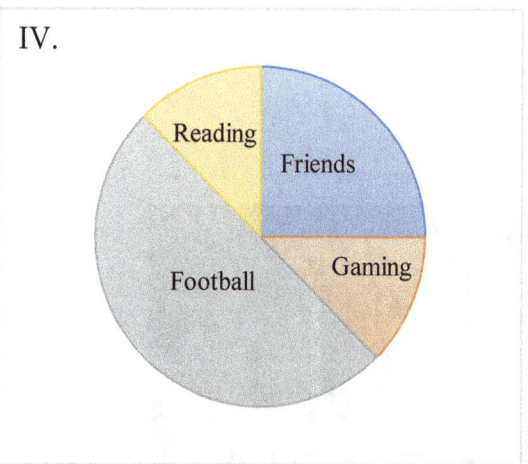

- Most children's favourite way to spend their spare time was playing with friends.
- The same number of students chose reading as those who chose playing video games.
- Fewer students chose reading than those who chose playing football.

38. Which chart shows the information correctly?

    A. chart I   C. chart III

    B. chart II   D. chart IV

The diagram below shows 2 rectangular boxes and a small cube.

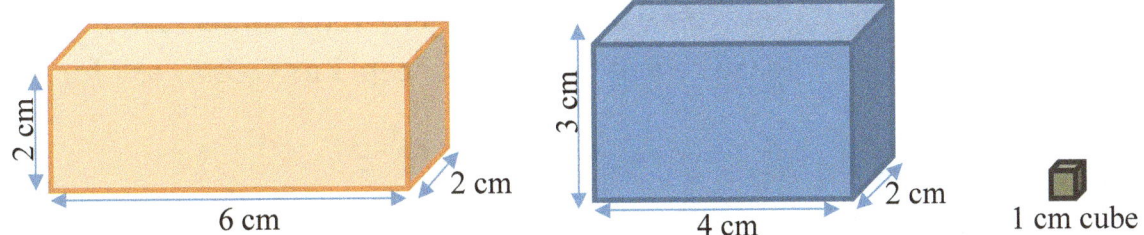

39. Using the information given, which of the following statements is correct?
    A. The orange box can hold the same number of 1 cm cubes as the blue box.
    B. The orange box can hold a greater number of 1 cm cubes than the blue box.
    C. The orange box can hold a smaller number of 1 cm cubes than the blue box.
    D. It is impossible to determine the answer based on the information given.

40. The diagram below shows how Sarah spent her pocket money last month.

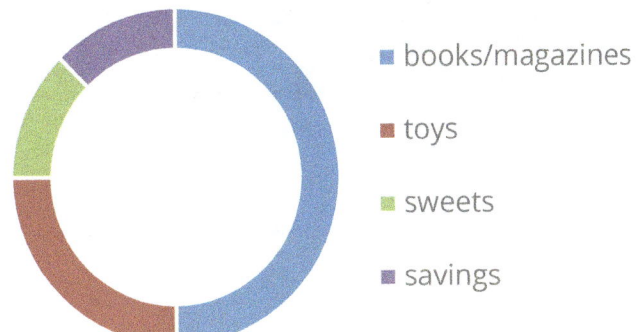

If Sarah spent $150 on sweets, how much money did she spend on books and magazines?

    A. $300
    B. $450
    C. $600
    D. $750

My evaluation of the test:_____

What is my plan of action? What will I do next?

....
....
....
....
....
....

40-QUESTIONS TEST #4

Are you getting better at being focused? Are you understanding why you got some of the questions wrong? Ready for another test? Let's go. Let's go. Let's prep for PEP and life.

40-QUESTIONS TEST #5
ANSWER SHEET

The next page has an answer sheet that you will use to record your answers. It is similar to the one you will most likely use during your PEP exams. Please remove this page.

(OPTIONAL HELPFUL INFORMATION)

TEST #: _____

START TIME: _____

END TIME: _____

SCORE: _____

Start this test whenever you are told to do so or whenever you are ready.

40–QUESTIONS TEST #5

Name: _____ ID no. _____ Age: ___

School: _____ School address: _____

1	Ⓐ	Ⓑ	Ⓒ	Ⓓ		21	Ⓐ	Ⓑ	Ⓒ	Ⓓ
2	Ⓐ	Ⓑ	Ⓒ	Ⓓ		22	Ⓐ	Ⓑ	Ⓒ	Ⓓ
3	Ⓐ	Ⓑ	Ⓒ	Ⓓ		23	Ⓐ	Ⓑ	Ⓒ	Ⓓ
4	Ⓐ	Ⓑ	Ⓒ	Ⓓ		24	Ⓐ	Ⓑ	Ⓒ	Ⓓ
5	Ⓐ	Ⓑ	Ⓒ	Ⓓ		25	Ⓐ	Ⓑ	Ⓒ	Ⓓ
6	Ⓐ	Ⓑ	Ⓒ	Ⓓ		26	Ⓐ	Ⓑ	Ⓒ	Ⓓ
7	Ⓐ	Ⓑ	Ⓒ	Ⓓ		27	Ⓐ	Ⓑ	Ⓒ	Ⓓ
8	Ⓐ	Ⓑ	Ⓒ	Ⓓ		28	Ⓐ	Ⓑ	Ⓒ	Ⓓ
9	Ⓐ	Ⓑ	Ⓒ	Ⓓ		29	Ⓐ	Ⓑ	Ⓒ	Ⓓ
10	Ⓐ	Ⓑ	Ⓒ	Ⓓ		30	Ⓐ	Ⓑ	Ⓒ	Ⓓ
11	Ⓐ	Ⓑ	Ⓒ	Ⓓ		31	Ⓐ	Ⓑ	Ⓒ	Ⓓ
12	Ⓐ	Ⓑ	Ⓒ	Ⓓ		32	Ⓐ	Ⓑ	Ⓒ	Ⓓ
13	Ⓐ	Ⓑ	Ⓒ	Ⓓ		33	Ⓐ	Ⓑ	Ⓒ	Ⓓ
14	Ⓐ	Ⓑ	Ⓒ	Ⓓ		34	Ⓐ	Ⓑ	Ⓒ	Ⓓ
15	Ⓐ	Ⓑ	Ⓒ	Ⓓ		35	Ⓐ	Ⓑ	Ⓒ	Ⓓ
16	Ⓐ	Ⓑ	Ⓒ	Ⓓ		36	Ⓐ	Ⓑ	Ⓒ	Ⓓ
17	Ⓐ	Ⓑ	Ⓒ	Ⓓ		37	Ⓐ	Ⓑ	Ⓒ	Ⓓ
18	Ⓐ	Ⓑ	Ⓒ	Ⓓ		38	Ⓐ	Ⓑ	Ⓒ	Ⓓ
19	Ⓐ	Ⓑ	Ⓒ	Ⓓ		39	Ⓐ	Ⓑ	Ⓒ	Ⓓ
20	Ⓐ	Ⓑ	Ⓒ	Ⓓ		40	Ⓐ	Ⓑ	Ⓒ	Ⓓ

Score _____ out of 40

www.mycheetahacademy.com

40-QUESTIONS TEST #5

Use the pattern shown to answer question 1.

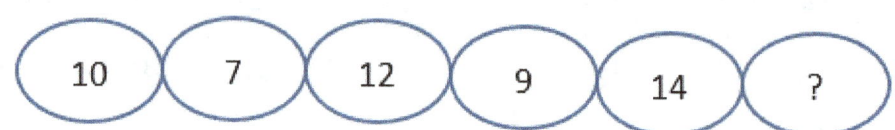

1. Which number comes next in the chain?

A. 7   B. 11   C. 10   D. 19

2. Nicolas estimated that there were 15,000 people at the New Year celebrations. Of the following numbers, which could **not** be the actual number of people at the event?

A. 14,561
B. 15,602
C. 14,899
D. 15,475

Below is a diagram of a regular hexagon (**EFGHIJ**).

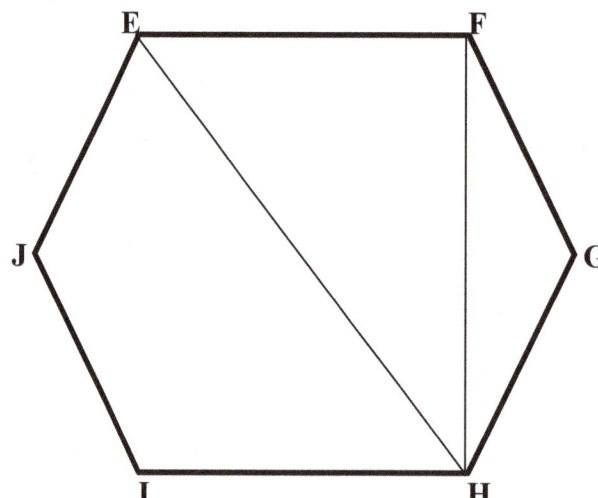

3. The greatest length is shown by which of the combined lengths?

A. EH + IJ
B. FH + EJ
C. FG + EF
D. FH + EH

4. Read the position of the arrow on this measuring cylinder. Choose the answer that best shows your reading.

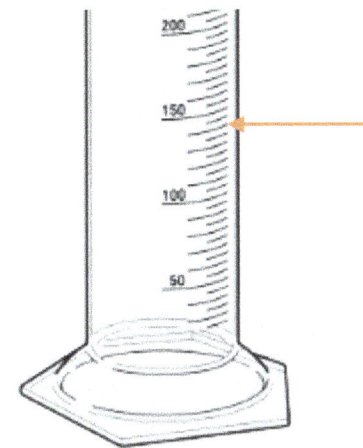

A. 140 units

B. 120 units

C. 130 units

D. 160 units

5. Choose the number that completes the following sequence:

5 | 15 | 35 | ? | 155 | 315

A. 50

B. 75

C. 95

D. 110

6.  is to  as 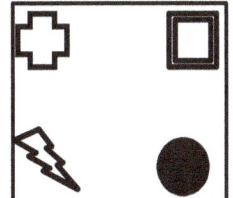 is to…

A.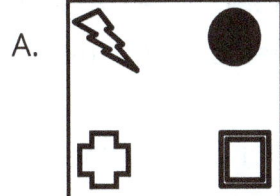

C.

B.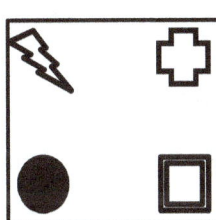

D.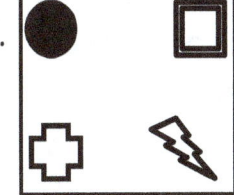

40-QUESTIONS TEST #5

7. Alan has invited his cousin, Thomas, to stay at his home. Alan lives with his father, Brian. Brian has one sibling, Amanda. Draw and use a family tree to tell which of the statements below **cannot** be correct?
   A. Thomas' mother is Brian's sister.
   B. Alan's aunt is Amanda.
   C. Thomas is Amanda's son.
   D. Thomas' father is Brian's brother.

For items 8 to 10, choose the best word to complete each statement.

8. Flooding has been caused by the _____ amount of rain this year.
   A. usual   C. tremendous
   B. towering   D. tiny

9. Many cultures _____ a leader.
   A. evict   C. edict
   B. elect   D. egret

10. The _____ sang beautifully.
   A. query   C. quire
   B. wire   D. choir

11. Gloria, Donald, Sonia and Errol were playing with a ten-sided die, numbered 0-9, taking turns to get the highest score. Gloria scored one less than Errol, who rolled the highest even number possible. Donald rolled an odd number less than 4, and Sonia's score was double that of Donald's. Which is the correct order of the children by score, from highest to lowest?
   A. Gloria, Sonia, Donald, Errol   C. Errol, Sonia, Donald, Gloria
   B. Errol, Gloria, Sonia, Donald   D. Donald, Errol, Gloria, Sonia

12. A fishing boat has a crew of 2 people and will carry a total of 8 people at any one time. How many trips will be needed to carry 40 passengers from Union Island to Carriacou?
   A. 5   B. 6   C. 7   D. 8

40-QUESTIONS TEST #5

Below are two boxes, each containing an extract. Read the texts, then decide whether the conclusions reached in questions 13 and 14 are true, false, partially true or unable to tell.

Extract 1

Did you know that a whopping 30% of Jamaica's land is covered in trees? Over 1000 species of trees exist there, including the Blue Mahoe which is the national tree of Jamaica.

Jamaica's forestry department is responsible for the management and conservation of 117,000 hectares of the country's forests. They also work with communities to plant trees and educate the population on sustainability.

Extract 2

Indonesia is a country located in Southeast Asia. Around 52% of Indonesia is forested, with many plantations producing palm oil to export around the world.

Indonesia's tropical rainforests are also world famous, providing homes to birds of paradise, Sumatran tigers and orangutans! It is therefore important to protect these rare habitats from deforestation.

13. Oil palm trees grow in Indonesia.
    A. true
    B. false
    C. partially true
    D. unable to tell

14. Jamaica has fewer trees than Indonesia.
    A. true
    B. false
    C. partially true
    D. unable to tell

For items 15 and 16, choose the word that is an essential part of the word in capital letters.

15. ORCHESTRA
    A. violin
    B. stage
    C. musicians
    D. sheet music

16. HURRICANE
    A. snow
    B. damage
    C. clouds
    D. wind

17. A local car park has 24 cars. All the cars are either black or white. There are two times as many black cars as there are white cars. How many black cars are in the car park?

A. 14 B. 16 C. 8 D. 20

18. Each diagram below contains numbers that follow the same rule. Use the information in the first two diagrams to work out the missing number in the last diagram.

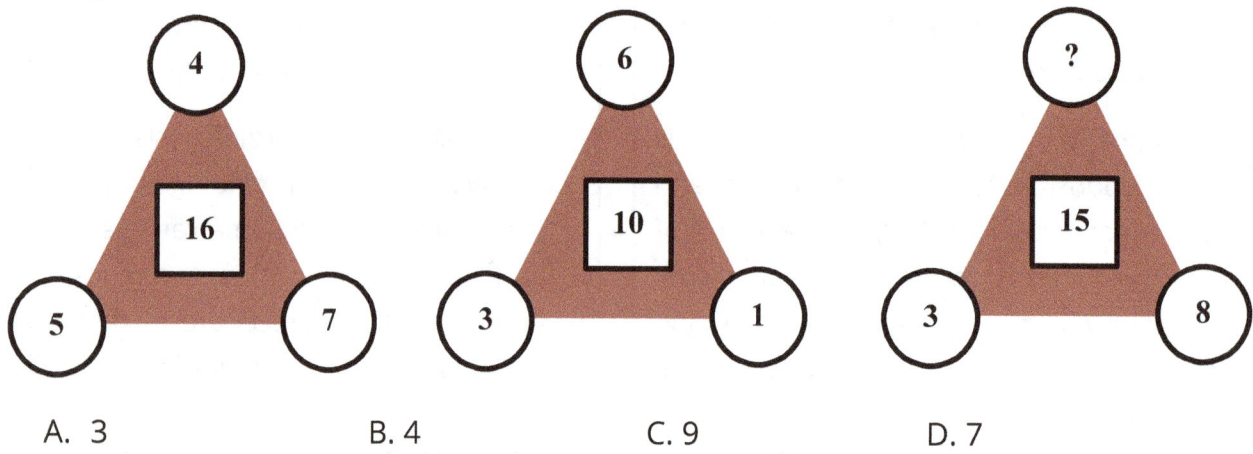

A. 3 B. 4 C. 9 D. 7

Use the pattern shown to answer question 19.

19. Which is the next shape in the pattern?

A. ⇨

B. △

C. ○

D. ▽

20. Choose the right option to complete the sequence.

never, sometimes, often, _____

A. occasionally
B. time
C. always
D. now

For items 21–23 below, choose the word that DOES NOT fit the group.

21. A. paper
B. pencil
C. spoon
D. ink

22. A. fly
B. walk
C. hover
D. glide

23. A. bully
B. torment
C. cuddle
D. harass

24. The diagram below shows the net of a geometric shape. Name the shape that is produced when the net is folded.

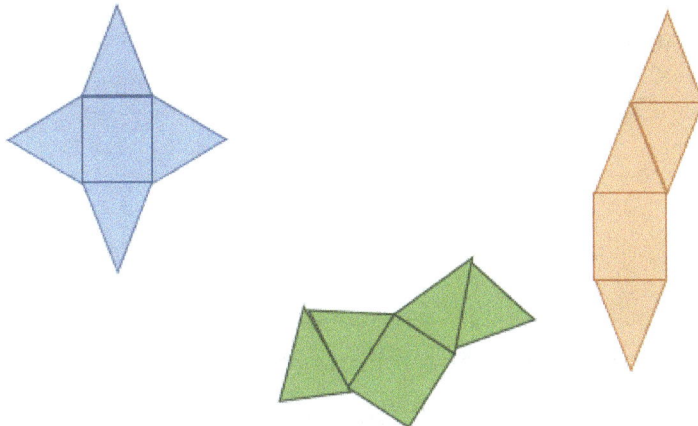

A. triangular-based pyramid
B. cuboid
C. square-based pyramid
D. trapezium

The diagram below shows the pets owned by children of a local school.

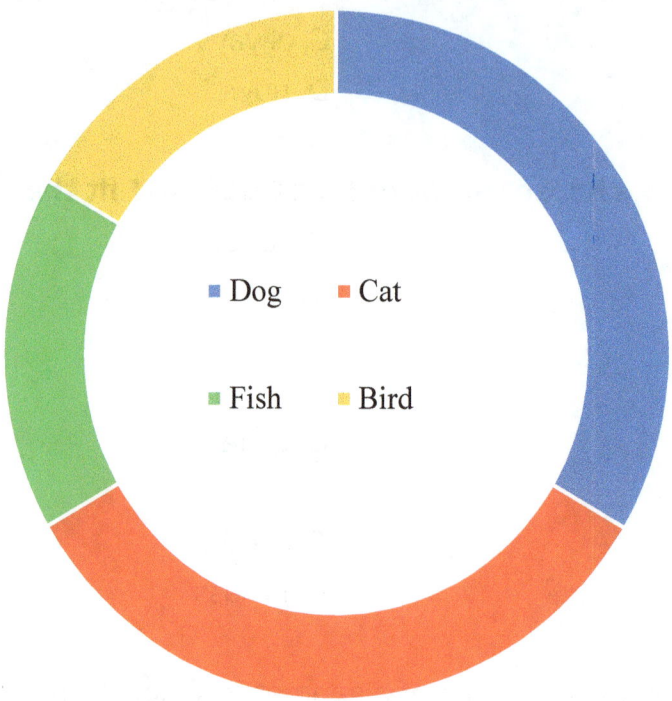

25. There are equal numbers of birds and fish and equal numbers of cats and dogs. Also, the number of dogs is twice the number of fish. If 32 children have a pet dog, how many students in the school own pets?
    A. 32
    B. 96
    C. 64
    D. 108

26. Kate wants to estimate how many crates she will need to hold 500 mangoes. What information is necessary for her to reach a conclusion?
    A. the number of crates she has
    B. the weight of a mango
    C. the number of mangoes that will be placed into one crate
    D. the average size of a mango

Look at the triangles in the box below. Alyssa has shown the information on a chart.

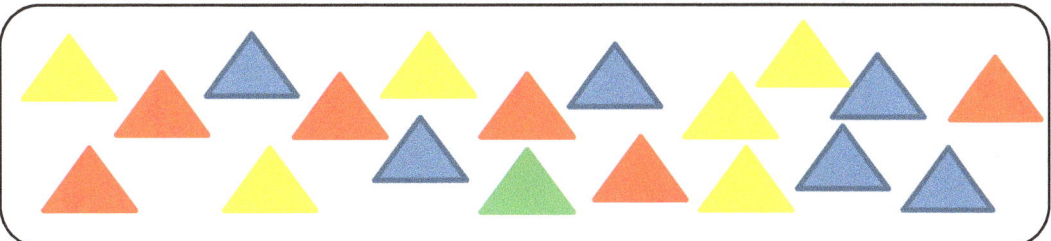

I.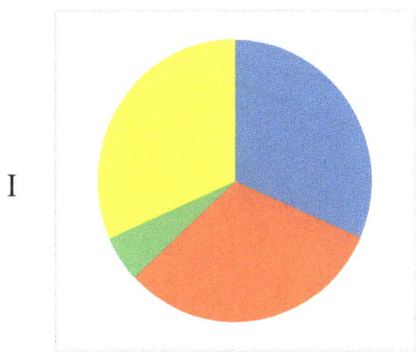

II.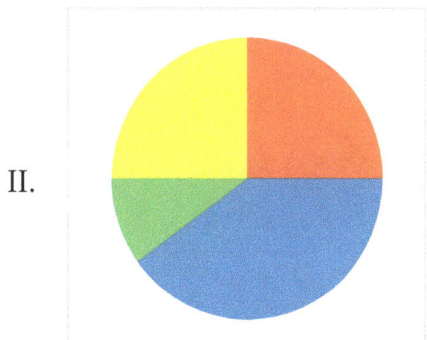

III.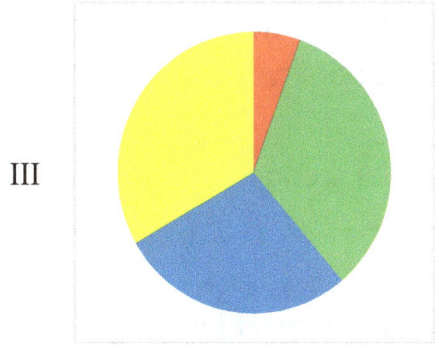

IV.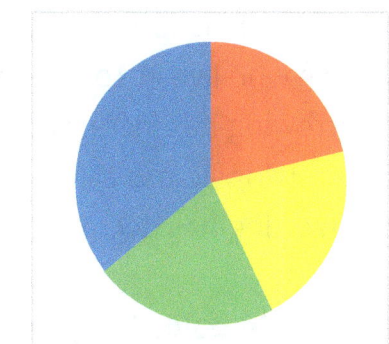

27. Which chart shows the information correctly?
A. chart I
B. chart II
C. chart III
D. chart IV

Look at the graph below. It shows the number of books borrowed from 4 libraries in Jamaican towns over a year.

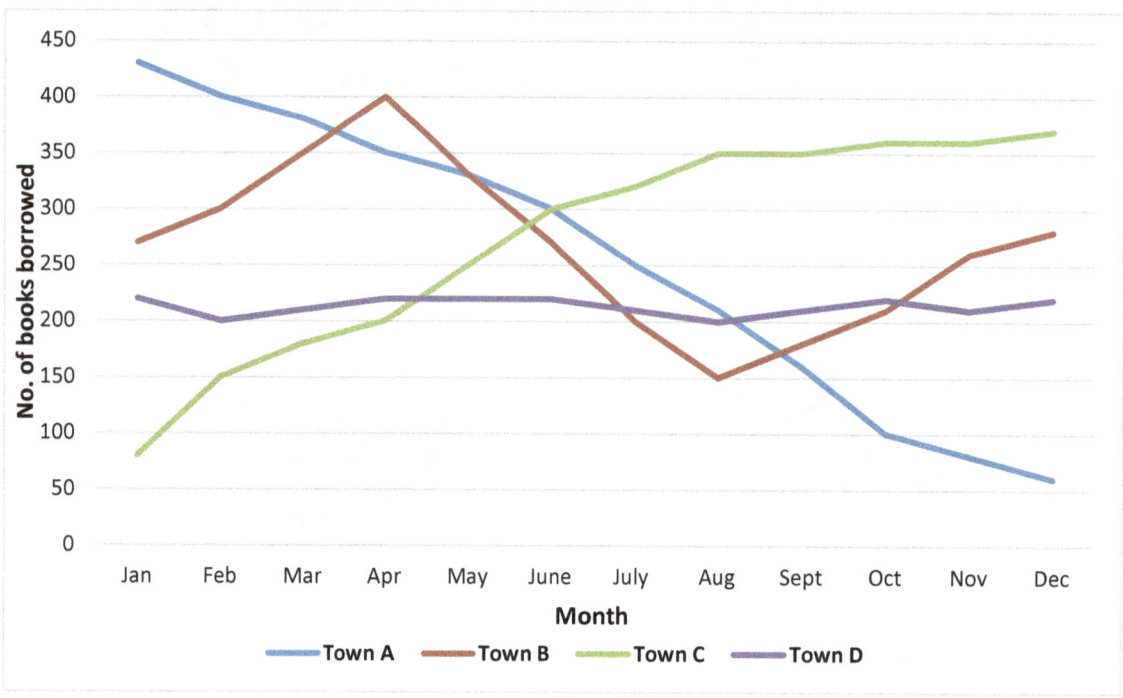

28. Based on the information shown in the graph, which conclusion is true?
    A. The people who live in Town B borrow the most books.
    B. Book borrowing has increased in Town D.
    C. Book borrowing across all 4 towns follows similar trends.
    D. Book borrowing has decreased in Town A.

Look at the words in bold. They are taken from an invented language. Next to each word is its English meaning.

      hurlftteut   means cook dinner
      seryteut   means delicious dinner
      jopuphurlft means vegetarian cook

29. Which word may mean cook fish?
    A. jopupteut
    B. hurlftgifik
    C. seryjopup
    D. gifikteut

Read the passage below before completing items 30 to 32.

On the south-west coast of Jamaica, where rivers feed into wetlands, you may be lucky enough to spot a manatee. You'll certainly know if you see one, because these creatures average 10 feet long and 1,200 pounds!

Commonly known as a 'sea cow', a manatee will spend 5 to 8 hours a day <u>grazing</u>, mostly on seagrass, just like a cow. In fact, a manatee can eat a whopping 5 to 10% of its bodyweight every single day.

These mostly <u>herbivorous</u> aquatic mammals spend their time eating, resting and travelling for their lifespan of 60 years or more. While this amazing creature has no natural predators, it is an endangered species due to the effects of humans on its habitat. For this reason, it is up to us to help the manatee.

30. _____ means the same as grazing.
    A. sleeping   C. guzzling
    B. feeding   D. rolling

40-QUESTIONS TEST #5

31. Which statement about the manatee is **not** true?
  A. The manatee lives where rivers meet wetlands.
  B. A manatee can grow about 10 feet long and weigh 1,200 lbs.
  C. A manatee spends 5 to 8 hours per day eating seagrass.
  D. The manatee has many natural predators.

32. Which of the following statements expresses the opinion of the writer?
  A. The manatee species has a lifespan of up to 60 years or more.
  B. The manatee eats 5 to 10% of its body weight each day.
  C. The manatee eats a lot each day.
  D. The manatee is an amazing creature.

33. Damon is looking for a page in a book. He notices that page 3 is a right-hand page. When he turns the page over, page 4 is on the left-hand side and faces page 5, on the right. Which of the following pairs of pages will also face each other?
  A. 16 and 17
  B. 9 and 10
  C. 17 and 18
  D. 21 and 22

34. If two numbers add to give 8 and their difference is 2, which pair of answers could be the two numbers
  A. 5 and 3
  B. 2 and 6
  C. 7 and 1
  D. 4 and 4

35. Look closely at the passage. Fill in the missing words in the correct order by choosing the most logical sequence.

Paul woke at _____ the next _____. He went to school and played football in the afternoon until _____. At _____, he did his homework and prepared for classes the next day.
  A. day, sunrise, sunset, night
  B. night, sunset, day, sunrise
  C. sunset, night, day, sunrise
  D. sunrise, day, sunset, night

In a survey, 100 Grade 6 students were asked how many brothers and sisters they had.

- Most students had no brothers or sisters.
- Half the number of students who had siblings had one brother or sister.
- The same number of students had two siblings as those who had three siblings.

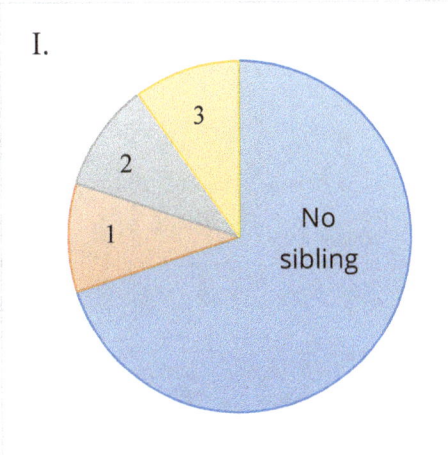
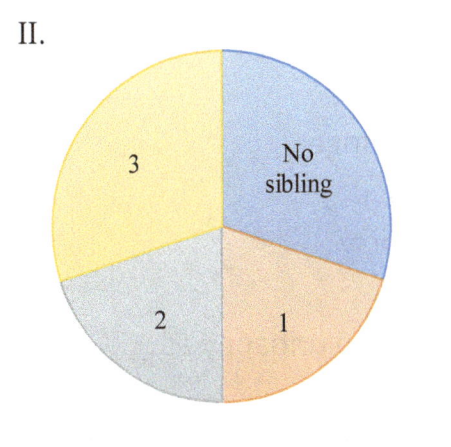
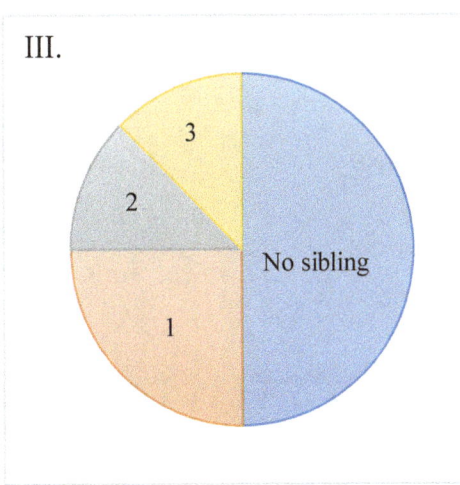
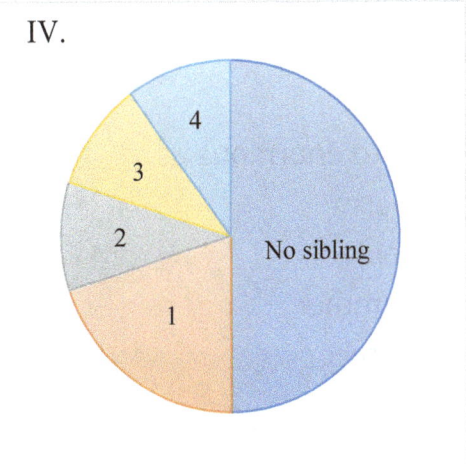

36. Which chart shows the information correctly?
   A. chart I
   B. chart II
   C. chart III
   D. chart IV

40-QUESTIONS TEST #5

For items 37 to 40, choose the word that best completes the sentence.

37. Bird is to flock as _____ is to pack.

    A. suitcase

    B. cat

    C. wolf

    D. cow

38. Car is to garage as _____ is to kitchen.

    A. stove

    B. lounge

    C. bed

    D. lorry

39. Sad is to unhappy as _____ is to hide.

    A. reveal

    B. seek

    C. conceal

    D. hidden

40. Big is to enormous as _____ is to freezing.

    A. warm

    B. cold

    C. summer

    D. rain

EVALUATE YOUR WORK!

Remember to evaluate your work and ask someone to evaluate it for you. If you don't understand, then please review the key concepts as well as ask for help.

- Got it!
- Almost got it!
- Don't understand.

My evaluation of the test:_____

What is my plan of action? What will I do next?

....
....
....
....
....
....
....

40-QUESTIONS TEST #6
ANSWER SHEET

The next page has an answer sheet that you will use to record your answers. It is similar to what you will most likely use during your PEP exams. Please remove this page.

(OPTIONAL HELPFUL INFORMATION)

TEST #: _____

START TIME: _____

END TIME: _____

SCORE: _____

Start this test whenever you are told to do so or whenever you are ready.

40-QUESTIONS TEST #6

Name: _____ ID no. _____ Age: ____

School: _____ School address: _____

1	Ⓐ	Ⓑ	Ⓒ	Ⓓ		21	Ⓐ	Ⓑ	Ⓒ	Ⓓ
2	Ⓐ	Ⓑ	Ⓒ	Ⓓ		22	Ⓐ	Ⓑ	Ⓒ	Ⓓ
3	Ⓐ	Ⓑ	Ⓒ	Ⓓ		23	Ⓐ	Ⓑ	Ⓒ	Ⓓ
4	Ⓐ	Ⓑ	Ⓒ	Ⓓ		24	Ⓐ	Ⓑ	Ⓒ	Ⓓ
5	Ⓐ	Ⓑ	Ⓒ	Ⓓ		25	Ⓐ	Ⓑ	Ⓒ	Ⓓ
6	Ⓐ	Ⓑ	Ⓒ	Ⓓ		26	Ⓐ	Ⓑ	Ⓒ	Ⓓ
7	Ⓐ	Ⓑ	Ⓒ	Ⓓ		27	Ⓐ	Ⓑ	Ⓒ	Ⓓ
8	Ⓐ	Ⓑ	Ⓒ	Ⓓ		28	Ⓐ	Ⓑ	Ⓒ	Ⓓ
9	Ⓐ	Ⓑ	Ⓒ	Ⓓ		29	Ⓐ	Ⓑ	Ⓒ	Ⓓ
10	Ⓐ	Ⓑ	Ⓒ	Ⓓ		30	Ⓐ	Ⓑ	Ⓒ	Ⓓ
11	Ⓐ	Ⓑ	Ⓒ	Ⓓ		31	Ⓐ	Ⓑ	Ⓒ	Ⓓ
12	Ⓐ	Ⓑ	Ⓒ	Ⓓ		32	Ⓐ	Ⓑ	Ⓒ	Ⓓ
13	Ⓐ	Ⓑ	Ⓒ	Ⓓ		33	Ⓐ	Ⓑ	Ⓒ	Ⓓ
14	Ⓐ	Ⓑ	Ⓒ	Ⓓ		34	Ⓐ	Ⓑ	Ⓒ	Ⓓ
15	Ⓐ	Ⓑ	Ⓒ	Ⓓ		35	Ⓐ	Ⓑ	Ⓒ	Ⓓ
16	Ⓐ	Ⓑ	Ⓒ	Ⓓ		36	Ⓐ	Ⓑ	Ⓒ	Ⓓ
17	Ⓐ	Ⓑ	Ⓒ	Ⓓ		37	Ⓐ	Ⓑ	Ⓒ	Ⓓ
18	Ⓐ	Ⓑ	Ⓒ	Ⓓ		38	Ⓐ	Ⓑ	Ⓒ	Ⓓ
19	Ⓐ	Ⓑ	Ⓒ	Ⓓ		39	Ⓐ	Ⓑ	Ⓒ	Ⓓ
20	Ⓐ	Ⓑ	Ⓒ	Ⓓ		40	Ⓐ	Ⓑ	Ⓒ	Ⓓ

Score _____ out of 40

www.mycheetahacademy.com

CHEETAH™ Toys & More, LLC Copyright 2022 © Copying is NOT allowed

Connect to **H**igher **E**ducation, **E**lectronic **T**ools, **A**plication and **H**elp

40-QUESTIONS TEST #6

For items 1 and 2, choose the word that is an essential part of the word in capital letters.

1. GUITAR
    A. strings
    B. plectrum
    C. musician
    D. sound

2. MEAL
    A. drink
    B. bread
    C. cutlery
    D. food

3. Look closely at the words in the box, then choose the logical sequence.

   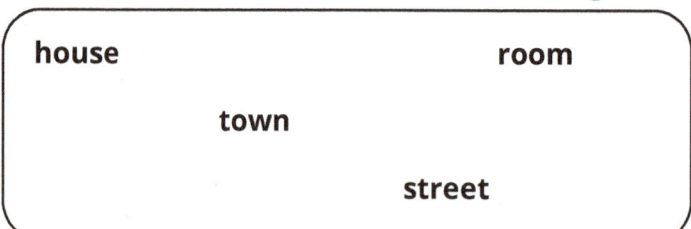

    A. room, house, street, town
    B. house, street, town, room
    C. town, street, room, house
    D. street, town, house, room

4. A plane has a crew of 5 people and can carry a total of 28 people at any one time. How many trips will be needed to carry 100 passengers from Havana to Kingston?
    A. 3
    B. 4
    C. 5
    D. 6

40–QUESTIONS TEST #6

5. Justin is 2 years older than Tianna was 3 years ago. Tianna is 2 years older than Devan. Devan is 10 years old. Amoy is 3 years older than Devan. Which is the correct order of the children by age, from youngest to oldest?
    A. Devan, Justin, Tianna, Amoy
    B. Amoy, Devan, Justin, Tianna
    C. Justin, Tianna, Amoy, Devan
    D. Tianna, Justin, Devan, Amoy

Below are two boxes, each containing an extract. Read then answer the questions.

Extract 1

In the Northwest Pacific Basin, hurricanes are known as typhoons. Here, there is no official typhoon season, as these storms form throughout the year.

This is the most active of all the Earth's basins, with an average of 16 typhoons per year. China, the Philippines, Japan, Korea, and Thailand are just some of the countries who jointly monitor activity in the area to issue warnings of a storm's approach.

Extract 2

Jamaica lies within the Atlantic Basin, which puts the island at risk of experiencing hurricanes between June 1 and November 30 every year.

While tropical storms can cause flooding and landslides, a named hurricane only hits the island every 10-11 years. Jamaica has avoided many storms that have reached nearby islands and is statistically less likely to take a direct hit.

6. Which of the following countries would not experience a typhoon?
    A. Japan
    B. Jamaica
    C. Philippines
    D. unable to tell

7. Choose the statement that BEST describes the information in the extracts.

   A. The storm season in Jamaica and the Northwest Pacific Basin are equally long.
   B. The storms are seasonal in Jamaica, while they are all year round in the Northwest Pacific Basin.
   C. Typhoons and hurricanes are the same.
   D. Jamaica is statistically less likely to get a hurricane.

The diagram below shows a cube and three nets.

8. Using the information given, which of the following statements is correct?
   A. All three nets can be folded to make a cube.
   B. None of the three nets can be folded to make a cube.
   C. Only the purple net can be folded to make a cube.
   D. Only the red net can be folded to make a cube.

9. Lucinda has bought tickets for the movie theatre. There are 12 seats in each row at the cinema, and seats 1 to 12 are in the first row, closest to the screen. If Lucinda's ticket is for seat number 79, in which row will she be sitting?
   A. the fifth row
   B. the sixth row
   C. the seventh row
   D. the eighth row

10. Circle the most suitable answer.

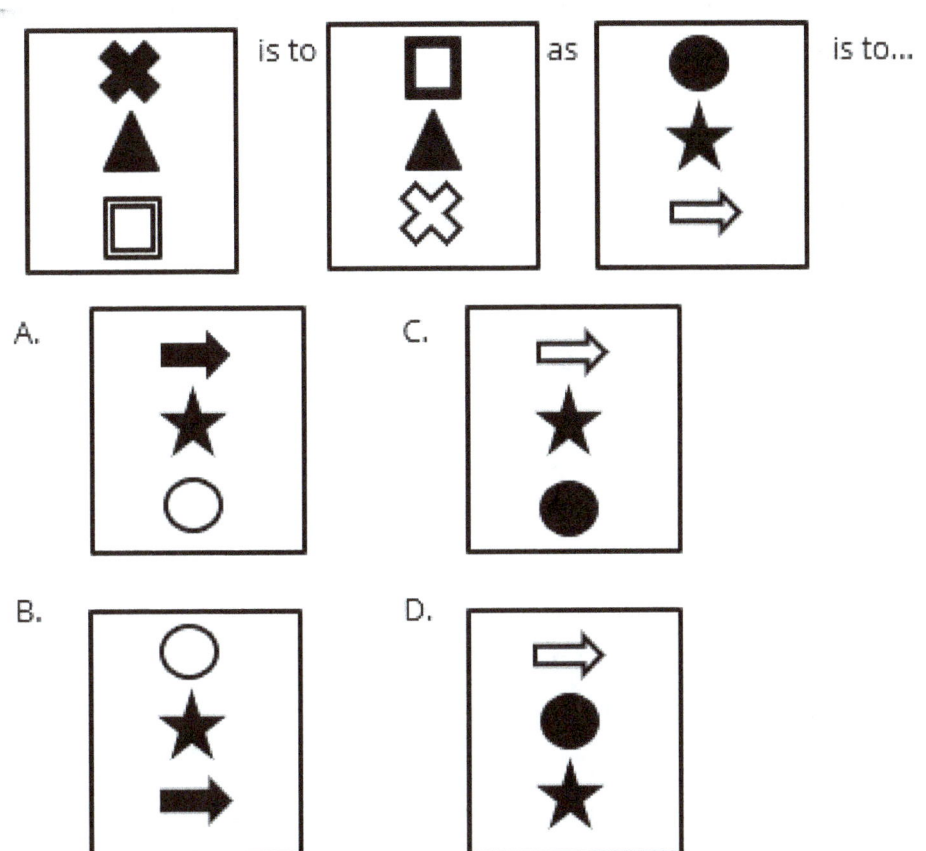

The diagram below shows the types of books borrowed from the school library.

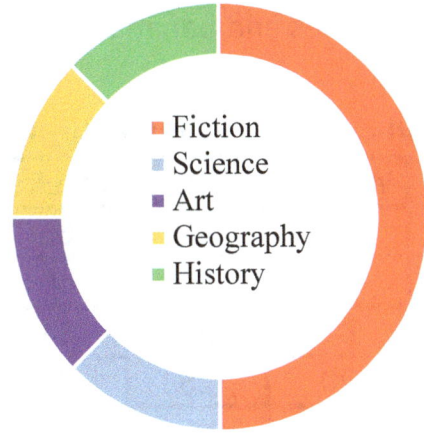

11. If 44 fiction books were borrowed, how many of the borrowed books were about art?

A. 8　　　　　B. 10　　　　　C. 9　　　　　D. 11

40–QUESTIONS TEST #6

12. A factory manager wants to know how many laptops a machine can make in an 8-hour shift. What information is necessary for him to reach a conclusion?
    A. the size of a laptop
    B. the time it takes to make one laptop
    C. the number of people who work per shift
    D. the materials required to make a laptop

13. Choose the right option to complete the sequence.
    mosquito, rabbit, elephant, _____
    A. whale   C. dog
    B. spider   D. tiger

Read the following statements:

      Bananas cost less than mangoes.
      Bananas cost more than coconuts.

14. If the first two statements are true, which of the following statements is also true?
    A. Bananas cost less than coconuts.
    B. Mangoes cost less than bananas.
    C. Mangoes cost more than bananas and coconuts.
    D. Coconuts cost more than mangoes and bananas.

The table below shows sweet sales at a local shop during the month of May.

Sweet	Week 1	Week 2	Week 3	Week 4
peppermint candy	58	40	62	70
coconut drops	32	54	40	55
stagga back	43	30	34	30
grater cake	20	26	35	42
peanut cake	44	41	53	30
tamarind balls	63	72	60	70

Use the information in the table to answer items 15 and 16.

15. Which week saw the highest sales of peanutcakes?
   A. week 1
   B. week 2
   C. week 3
   D. week 4

16. Which sweet increased the most in popularity when comparing sales from week 1 and week 4?
   A. grater cake
   B. coconut drops
   C. peppermint candy
   D. tamarind balls

17. Maria estimated that 100,000 attended Jamaica Carnival. Of the following numbers, which could **not** be the actual number of people at carnival?
   A. 99,367
   B. 99,781
   C. 99,562
   D. 100,498

Look at the graph below. It shows a market stall's fruit sales over the course of a month.

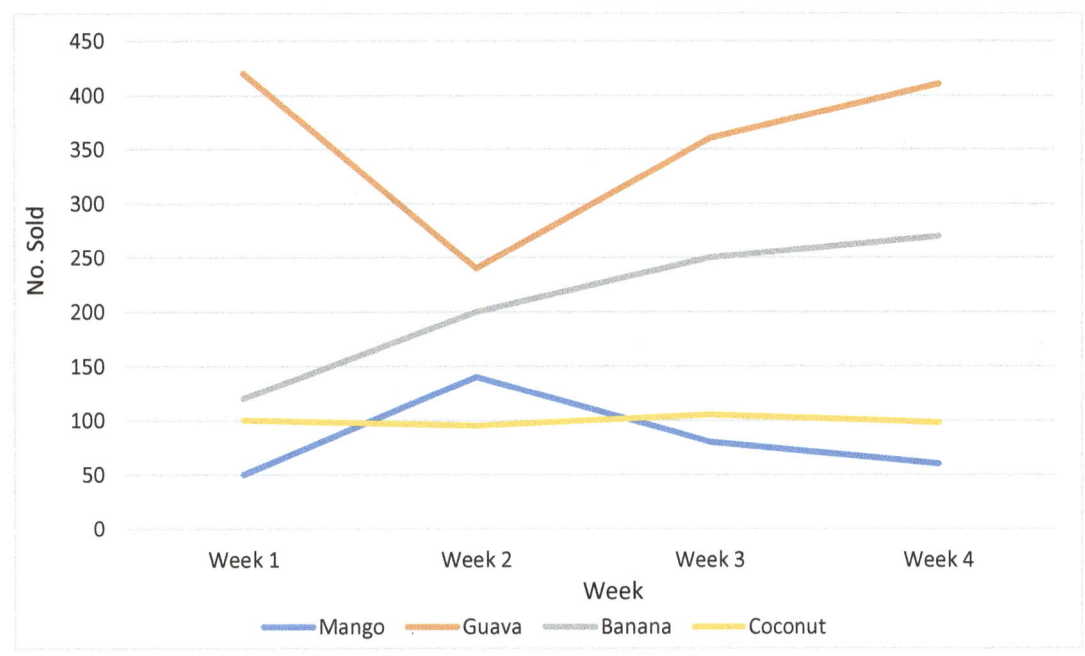

18. Based on the information shown in the graph, which conclusion is true?

   A. More coconuts were sold than mangoes.

   B. Banana sales decreased throughout the month.

   C. There was a sharp drop in guava sales in week 3.

   D. Coconut sales remained steady throughout the month.

Look at the words in bold. They are taken from an invented language. Next to each word is its English meaning.

ghedkriidr	means face forward
pahftriidr	means centre forward
asdonghedk	means smiley face

19. Which word may mean facemask?

   A. asdonwkftjj   C. ghedkscvvpo

   B. riidrpahft   D. pahftghedk

For items 20 to 23, choose the word that best completes the sentence.

20. Grass is to green as _____ is to dry.

   A. water   C. yellow

   B. desert   D. wet

21. Eat is to ate as _____ is to bought.

   A. buy   C. shop

   B. carried   D. sell

22. Plant is to grow as _____ is to burn.

   A. tree   C. forest

   B. wood   D. fire

23. Graceful is to clumsy as _____ is to cry.

   A. laugh   C. sob

   B. upset   D. tears

24. Choose the numbers that complete the following sequence:

102 | 86 | ? | 54 | ? | 22 | 6

A. 70, 40

B. 72, 42

C. 70, 38

D. 68, 44

Read the passage below before answering items 25, 26 and 27.

Blue Mountain coffee is one of the most **sought-after** coffees in the world. Grown in a specially designated area of the longest mountain range in Jamaica, the combination of soil and climate provides perfect conditions for the unmistakable aroma. Its flavour is smooth and delicate, well-deserving of its reputation as the 'Champagne' of coffees.

As this coffee is considered one of the best in the world, it has become expensive and is exported across the globe. Japan is its greatest fan, buying 70% of the precious beans! Such is the love for the coffee in Japan, that there is an **annual** Jamaica Blue Mountain Coffee Day to celebrate the product first arriving on its shores in 1953.

25. Which word means the same as 'annual'?

A. official

B. fun

C. famous

D. yearly

26. Which of the following could also be considered 'sought-after'?

A. bread

B. diamonds

C. water

D. books

27. Which of the following statements expresses the opinion of the writer?

A. Blue Mountain coffee is smooth and delicate.

B. Blue Mountain coffee is too expensive.

C. Japan buys too much Blue Mountain coffee.

D. People should not believe that Blue Mountain coffee is one of the best.

28. Look at the pattern shown below. Use the first two rows to work out the missing number in the third row.

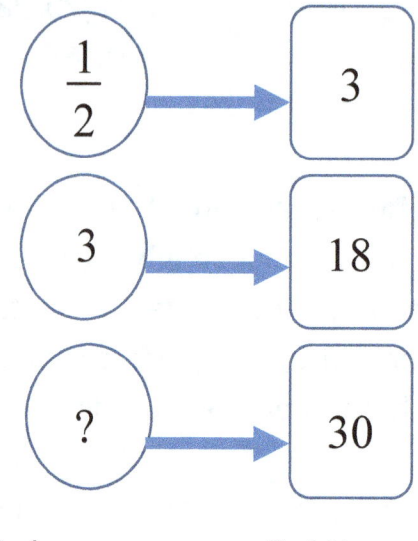

A. 5 B. 4 C. 4 ½ D. 6

Look at the number in the circle shown. Subtract 21.

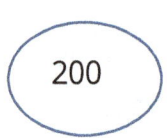

29. What is the place value of the digit 7 in the answer?
 A. tens C. hundreds
 B. tenths D. hundredths

30. What is the approximate value at the dot on the number line shown?

A. 2.25 B. 2.75 C. 1.95 D. 2.50

For items 31 to 33, choose the word that does not fit the group.
31. A. squeak

B. cheep

C. tweet

D. roar

32. A. rain

B. sunshine

C. hail

D. snow

33. A. leap

B. bound

C. crouch

D. spring

Below is a diagram of a trapezium (**RSTU**).

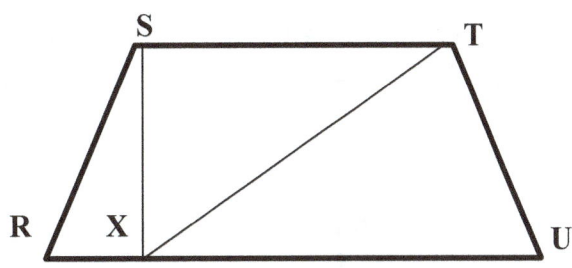

34. The shortest length is shown by which of the following?

A. ST + TU

B. SX + RX

C. RX + XT

D. XU + SR

35. John's father is Tom's uncle. Mary is John's sister. What is the relationship between Tom and Mary?

A. siblings

B. uncle and niece

C. cousins

D. father and daughter

The growth stages of a chick are shown in the pictures below.

1.

2.
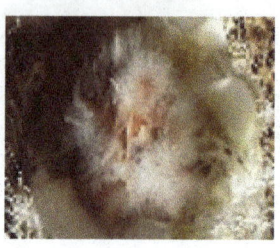
3.

4.

5.

36. Which of the following sequences puts the growth stages of a chick into logical order?

   A. 1, 4, 3, 5, 2   C. 2, 1, 3, 4, 5

   B. 5, 3, 1, 2, 4   D. 3, 5, 4, 2, 1

37. Each diagram below contains numbers that follow the same rule. Use the information in the first two diagrams to work out the missing number in the last diagram.

   A. 14   B. 8   C. 11   D. 13

For items 38 and 39, choose the best word to complete each statement.

38. Aspirin is a _____ for a headache.

   A. relay   C. remedy

   B. reality   D. rectify

39. The final _____ in the movie was shocking!

A. seen

B. scene

C. sean

D. seine

Use the pattern shown to answer this question.

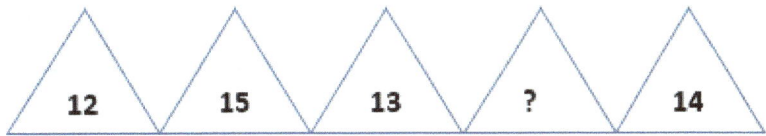

40. What is the next number in the chain?

A. 11

B. 12

C. 17

D. 16

40-QUESTIONS TEST #6

I have a special assignment for you. Work with your peer (another student) to review each other's responses for the next set of questions.

What exactly will you be doing? You will be reviewing and critiquing how the other person responded to the questions and then provide feedback. Here are some suggestions for giving useful feedback:

1. Review one test at a time.

2. Spend a few minutes to review all the answers.

3. Explain your partner's strengths and weaknesses. What did the person do well and what could be improved?

4. Offer any suggestions, for example study tips or concepts that your peer may be missing.

5. Be as clear and specific as possible.

6. Be courteous and kind; don't be rude with your feedback.

7. Refer to any additional resources, for example your textbook, for any concept that is unclear to you both.

8. Have fun and learn from each other.

www.mycheetahacademy.com

EVALUATE YOUR WORK!

Remember to evaluate your work and ask someone to evaluate it for you. If you don't understand, then please review the key concepts as well as ask for help.

- 😊 Got it!
- 😐 Almost got it!
- ☹️ Don't understand.

My evaluation of the test:_____

What is my plan of action? What will I do next?

40-QUESTIONS TEST #7
ANSWER SHEET

The next page has an answer sheet that you will use to record your answers. It is similar to what you will most likely use during your PEP exams. Please remove this page.

(OPTIONAL HELPFUL INFORMATION)

TEST #: _____

START TIME: _____

END TIME: _____

SCORE: _____

Start this test whenever you are told to do so or whenever you are ready.

40-QUESTIONS TEST #7

Name: _____   ID no. _____   Age: ___

School: _____   School address: _____

1	Ⓐ	Ⓑ	Ⓒ	Ⓓ	21	Ⓐ	Ⓑ	Ⓒ	Ⓓ
2	Ⓐ	Ⓑ	Ⓒ	Ⓓ	22	Ⓐ	Ⓑ	Ⓒ	Ⓓ
3	Ⓐ	Ⓑ	Ⓒ	Ⓓ	23	Ⓐ	Ⓑ	Ⓒ	Ⓓ
4	Ⓐ	Ⓑ	Ⓒ	Ⓓ	24	Ⓐ	Ⓑ	Ⓒ	Ⓓ
5	Ⓐ	Ⓑ	Ⓒ	Ⓓ	25	Ⓐ	Ⓑ	Ⓒ	Ⓓ
6	Ⓐ	Ⓑ	Ⓒ	Ⓓ	26	Ⓐ	Ⓑ	Ⓒ	Ⓓ
7	Ⓐ	Ⓑ	Ⓒ	Ⓓ	27	Ⓐ	Ⓑ	Ⓒ	Ⓓ
8	Ⓐ	Ⓑ	Ⓒ	Ⓓ	28	Ⓐ	Ⓑ	Ⓒ	Ⓓ
9	Ⓐ	Ⓑ	Ⓒ	Ⓓ	29	Ⓐ	Ⓑ	Ⓒ	Ⓓ
10	Ⓐ	Ⓑ	Ⓒ	Ⓓ	30	Ⓐ	Ⓑ	Ⓒ	Ⓓ
11	Ⓐ	Ⓑ	Ⓒ	Ⓓ	31	Ⓐ	Ⓑ	Ⓒ	Ⓓ
12	Ⓐ	Ⓑ	Ⓒ	Ⓓ	32	Ⓐ	Ⓑ	Ⓒ	Ⓓ
13	Ⓐ	Ⓑ	Ⓒ	Ⓓ	33	Ⓐ	Ⓑ	Ⓒ	Ⓓ
14	Ⓐ	Ⓑ	Ⓒ	Ⓓ	34	Ⓐ	Ⓑ	Ⓒ	Ⓓ
15	Ⓐ	Ⓑ	Ⓒ	Ⓓ	35	Ⓐ	Ⓑ	Ⓒ	Ⓓ
16	Ⓐ	Ⓑ	Ⓒ	Ⓓ	36	Ⓐ	Ⓑ	Ⓒ	Ⓓ
17	Ⓐ	Ⓑ	Ⓒ	Ⓓ	37	Ⓐ	Ⓑ	Ⓒ	Ⓓ
18	Ⓐ	Ⓑ	Ⓒ	Ⓓ	38	Ⓐ	Ⓑ	Ⓒ	Ⓓ
19	Ⓐ	Ⓑ	Ⓒ	Ⓓ	39	Ⓐ	Ⓑ	Ⓒ	Ⓓ
20	Ⓐ	Ⓑ	Ⓒ	Ⓓ	40	Ⓐ	Ⓑ	Ⓒ	Ⓓ

Score _____ out of 40

www.mycheetahacademy.com

40-QUESTIONS TEST #7

1. Nicola took a bus from Kingston to Ocho Rios. The bus left at 8:15 a.m. and was expected to take approximately 2 hours 45 minutes. Of the following arrival times, which is **unlikely** to be the actual arrival time in Ocho Rios?
   A. 11:00 a.m.
   B. 10:55 a.m.
   C. 10:30 a.m.
   D. 11:15 a.m.

2. A netball tournament is taking place at a local high school. Each team must consist of exactly 5 players and 1 coach to compete. Which of the numbers below could **not** be the number of people competing in the tournament?
   A. 42
   B. 54
   C. 30
   D. 45

For items 3 and 4, choose the word that is an essential part of the word in capital letters.

3. LANGUAGE
   A. text
   B. words
   C. tongue
   D. speech

4. HOSPITAL
   A. treatment
   B. nurse
   C. medication
   D. stethoscope

Look at the number in the circle shown. Add 487.

963

5. What is the place value of the digit 1 in the answer?
   A. tens
   B. thousands
   C. hundreds
   D. ten-thousands

40-QUESTIONS TEST #7

6. Look closely at the words in the box, then choose the logical sequence.

> cook   serve
> eat
> prepare

A. cook, prepare, serve, eat
B. prepare, cook, serve, eat
C. eat, cook, prepare, serve
D. prepare, eat, cook, serve

7. A student made these purchases at the bookshop: two books at a cost of $80 each, 2 pens at $40 each, 3 pencils at $20 each and 1 sharpener at $15. He gave the shopkeeper $500 for his purchase. How much change should he receive?

A. $185   B. $210   C. $295   D. $205

For items 8 to 11, choose the word that best completes the sentence.

8. Hand is to fingers as _____ is to pages.
A. paper   C. shelf
B. words   D. book

9. Lunch is to meal as _____ is to furniture.
A. table   C. food
B. wood   D. storage

10. Pen is to write as _____ is to cut.
A. fork   C. pencil
B. knife   D. snip

11. Hungry is to eat as _____ is to scratch.
A. food   C. itch
B. wound   D. nail

Below is a diagram of a kite (**JKLM**).

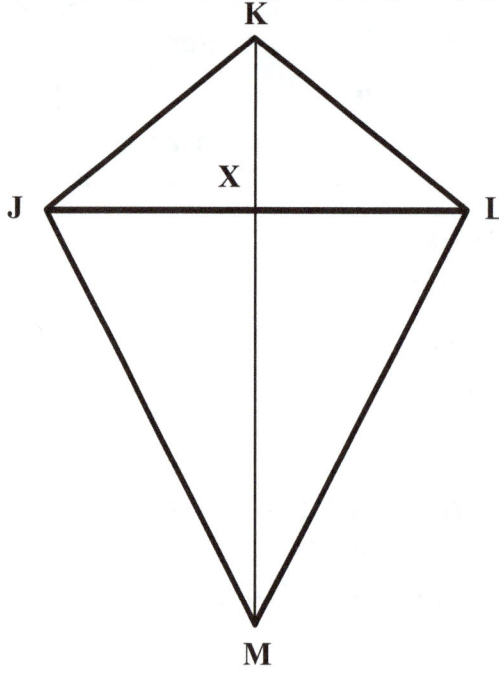

12. The greatest length is shown by which of the following?

    A. JL + KX
    B. JX + KJ
    C. JM + KM
    D. KJ + KL

13. A yacht has a crew of 3 people and can carry a total of 12 people at any one time. To make a profit, the yacht must charter enough trips to Negril Beach to take payment from 53 passengers. What is the minimum number of trips the yacht must make per week to make a profit?

    A. 4
    B. 5
    C. 6
    D. 7

The diagram below shows the location of Amelia in the town centre.

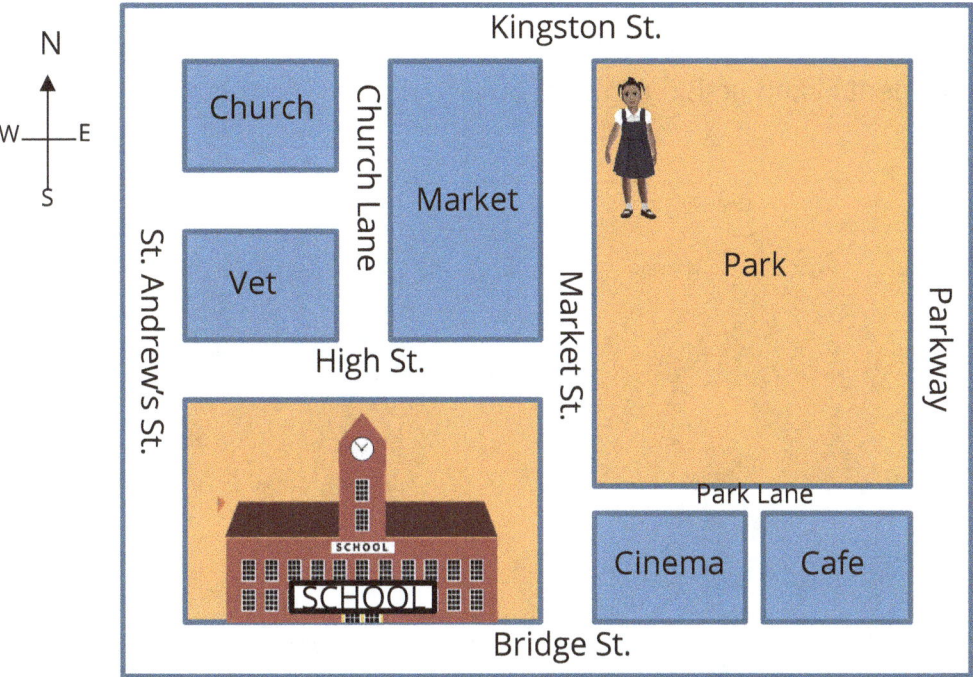

14. Using the information given, which of the following statements is correct?
    A. Amelia must head south on Market St. and east on Bridge St. to reach school.
    B. Amelia must head east on Kingston St. and south on Parkway to reach school.
    C. Amelia must head south on Market St. and west on High St. to reach school.
    D. Amelia must head south on Market St. and west on Bridge St. to reach school.

15. Cameron is reading an alphabet book to his younger sister. He notices that the letter 'A' appears on a left-hand page, and the letter 'B' is opposite, on the right-hand side. When he turns the page, the letter 'C' is on the left and faces the letter 'D' on the right. Which of the following pairs of letters will also face each other?
    A. F and G
    B. J and K
    C. P and Q
    D. U and V

In a survey, 100 Grade 6 students were asked what type of movie they like best.
- Very few students enjoyed dramas.
- More students preferred comedy to romance.
- Most students liked sci-fi movies.
- Other students liked action movies.

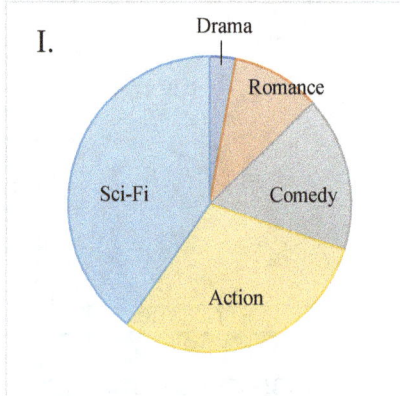
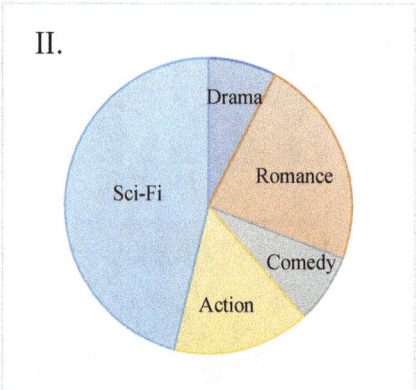
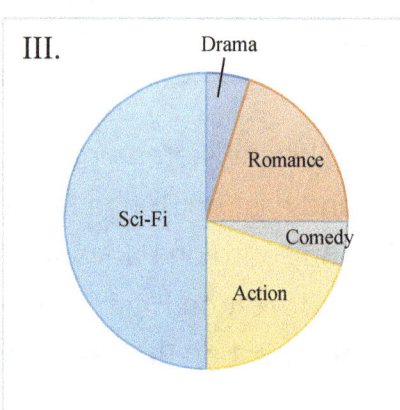
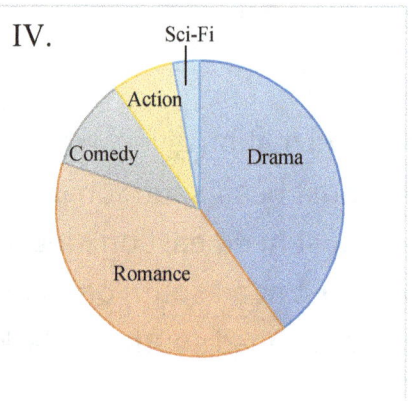

16. Which chart shows the information correctly?

A. chart I
B. chart II
C. chart III
D. chart IV

17. Choose the right option to complete the sequence.

letter, word, sentence _____

A. book
B. paragraph
C. page
D. alphabet

40-QUESTIONS TEST #7

Below are two boxes, each containing an extract. Read the texts, then complete items 18 and 19.

Extract 1

In the late 1700s, carnival began in Trinidad when the Spanish encouraged immigration to the island. Before Lent, the new settlers held masquerade balls while the slaves watched through windows. Soon, the slaves held celebrations of their own, which became their carnival of today.

After the slaves were freed in 1838, carnival became a show of liberation and strength. Today, the islanders of Trinidad and Tobago come together for a national holiday and plenty of fun!

Extract 2

In the 1940s, the University of the West Indies opened in Jamaica and the first signs of Carnival hit the island. The students from Trinidad and Tobago recreated their home festival on campus, and the seeds of the party were sewn.

Carnival began officially in 1990 and is a time to party! The fun begins as early as February, culminating in a spectacular road parade through Kingston.

18. Based on extracts 1 and 2, which statement best describes the history of carnival on both islands.
    A. Carnival, which involves parties and parades, was introduced to Trinidad and Tobago through migrants over 200 years before students from that country introduced the celebration to Jamaica.
    B. Carnival is a celebration of the liberation of the islanders of Trinidad and Tobago.
    C. In Jamaica, carnival is celebrated in February, and it culminates in a road parade.
    D. The Spanish introduced carnival to Trinidad and Tobago in 1700, and the students of the University of the West Indies introduced carnival to Jamaica in 1990.

19. In what year did Carnival begin in Jamaica?
    A. 1838
    B. 1990
    C. 1940
    D. 1700

The steps for growing corn are shown in the pictures below.

1.

2.

3.

4.

5.

20. Which of the following sequences puts the steps of growing corn into logical order?

   A. 4, 2, 1, 5, 3
   B. 3, 5, 4, 1, 2
   C. 2, 4, 5, 3, 1
   D. 2, 4, 1, 5, 3

21. Billy has ordered a tonne of bricks. He wants to know how many bricks he can expect to arrive. What information is necessary for him to reach a conclusion?
   A. the length and width of one brick
   B. the material a brick is made from
   C. the size of the pallet on which the bricks will arrive
   D. the weight of one brick

22. Double the product of 6 and 8, then add their sum. Which of the following is your answer to the nearest hundred?

   A. 90
   B. 110
   C. 100
   D. 120

40-QUESTIONS TEST #7

For items 23 to 25, choose the best word to complete each statement.

23. The police are doing all they can to _____ crime.
   A. instigate
   B. prevent
   C. launch
   D. inspire

24. My dog hurt his _____ .
   A. pause
   B. pours
   C. paws
   D. pores

25. The wave swept up and _____ the boat.
   A. capitalised
   B. capsized
   C. captioned
   D. capsuled

26. A box contains pens of four different colours. A third of the pens are black. The number of red pens is half the number of blue pens. There is an even number of green pens. Which of the following could **not** be the number of pens in the box?
   A. 15   B. 12   C. 9   D. 24

Look at the words in bold. They are taken from an invented language. Next to each word is its English meaning.

jlxatspacb	means waterproof tent
lisdspacb	means pitch tent
wueehlisds	means football pitch

27. Which word may mean pitchfork?
   A. lisdssjifd
   B. spacbwueeh
   C. jlxatlisds
   D. sjifdspacb

Look at the graph below. It shows the number of attendees at three local football clubs over a year.

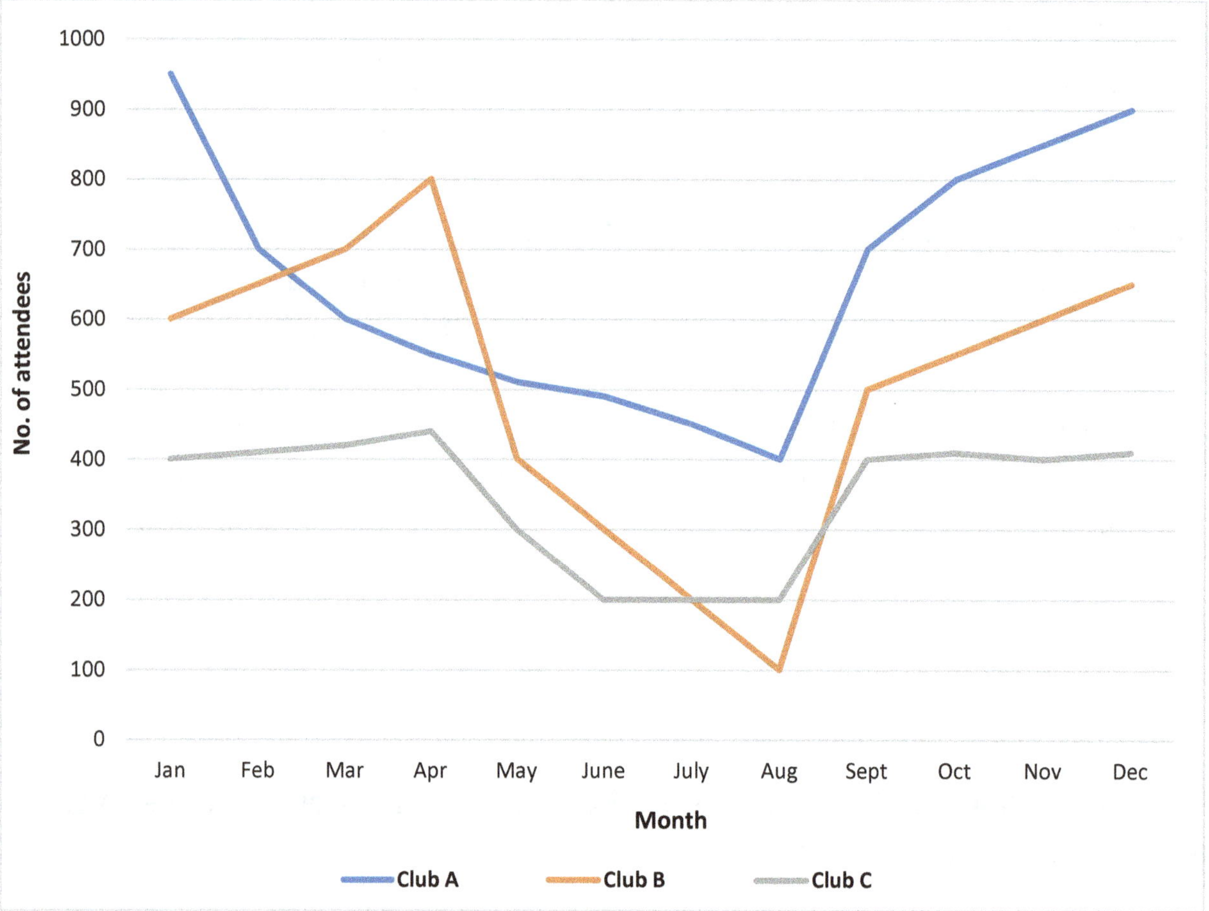

28. Based on the information shown in the graph, which conclusion is true?
    A. The number of attendees at club C remained constant throughout the year.
    B. Club B saw a sharp decrease in the number of attendees between May and August.
    C. The least popular football club is club A.
    D. December saw the lowest numbers of attendees at local football clubs.

The diagram below shows how local children travel to school.

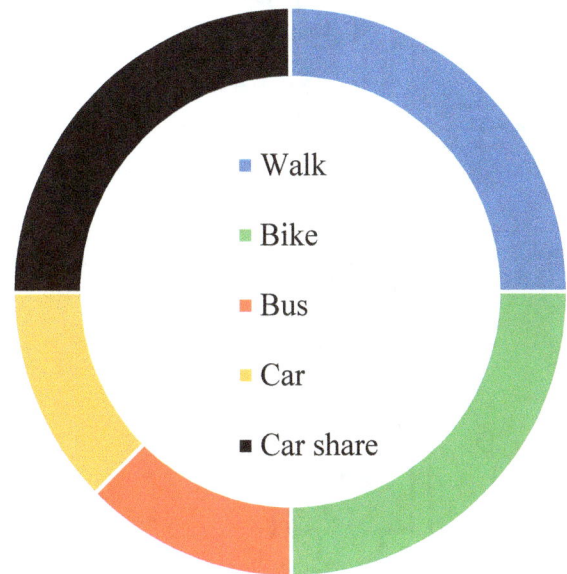

29. If 15 children travel by bus, how many children ride their bikes to school?

A. 25 B. 45 C. 30 D. 50

30. Carmen, Roy, Edward and Monica have a bike race to the shops. They all leave their houses at the same time. It takes Roy twice as long to ride to the shops as it takes Monica. Edward takes 2 minutes longer than Roy. Monica takes 5 minutes to ride from her house to the shops. Carmen takes 6 minutes less than Roy to get there. Which is the correct order of the children by arrival time at the shops, from first to last?

A. Monica, Carmen, Edward, Roy
B. Edward, Roy, Monica, Carmen
C. Carmen, Monica, Roy, Edward
D. Roy, Carmen, Edward, Monica

31. Circle the most suitable answer.

 is to  as 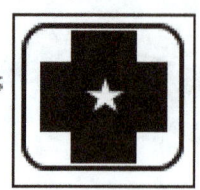 is to...

A.

C.

B.

D.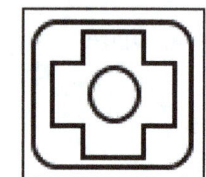

Read the passage below before answering items 32 to 34.

Ian Fleming was a British writer most famous for creating the British secret service agent, James Bond. Fleming created the character of Bond while staying at his gorgeous luxury villa in Ocho Rios, Jamaica.

Fleming designed the villa himself in 1946, after falling in love with Jamaica while he served on the island during WWII. Built on the edge of a cliff, overlooking a private beach, it was here that Fleming wrote all twelve Bond novels. Fleming would set himself a two-thousand word count each day and write at a table facing the wall, because he found the stunning Jamaican surroundings such a **distraction**!

Fleming's estate was named 'GoldenEye' after a war-time operation he oversaw as a

Naval Lieutenant-Commander. **Fittingly,** the name 'GoldenEye' was later used as the title for a 1995 Bond movie. As 'GoldenEye' was the seventeenth movie in the James Bond series, it used no story elements whatsoever from Fleming's novels.

32. Which word means the same as 'fittingly'?
    A. annoyingly
    B. unexpectedly
    C. suitably
    D. famously

33. Which of the following would Fleming MOST LIKELY consider a 'distraction'?
    A. beach
    B. phone
    C. silence
    D. furniture

34. Which of the following statements expresses the opinion of the writer?
    A. The bond novels are not very well known.
    B. 'GoldenEye' was a poor choice of name for the estate.
    C. Ian Fleming was popular with the people of Jamaica.
    D. Fleming's villa is a beautiful place.

35. Look at the pattern shown below. Use the first two rows to work out the missing number in the third row.

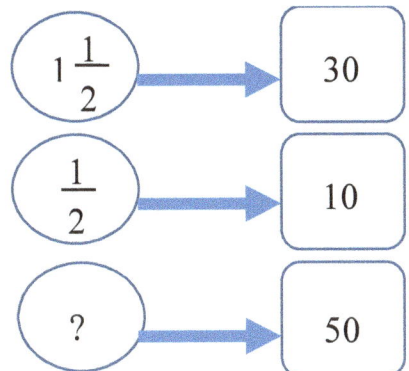

A. 2
B. 1
C. 2½
D. 3

For items 36 to 38, choose the word that does not fit the group.

36. A. fur
    B. fleece
    C. hair
    D. paw

37. A. heart
    B. skull
    C. kidney
    D. liver

38. A. touch
    B. smooth
    C. rough
    D. soft

The table below shows information about birds and their eggs. Use the information in the table to answer items 39 and 40.

Bird	Average weight (g)	Average egg length (mm)	Egg incubation period (days)
chicken	60	57	20
duck	80	76	27
hummingbird	30	13	16
mockingbird	50	25	12
ostrich	100	160	45

39. What is the difference in egg length between the second largest bird and the second smallest bird?

    A. 44 mm
    B. 51 mm
    C. 72 mm
    D. 63 mm

40. How many birds lay eggs which hatch within 3 weeks?

    A. 2
    B. 4
    C. 5
    D. 3

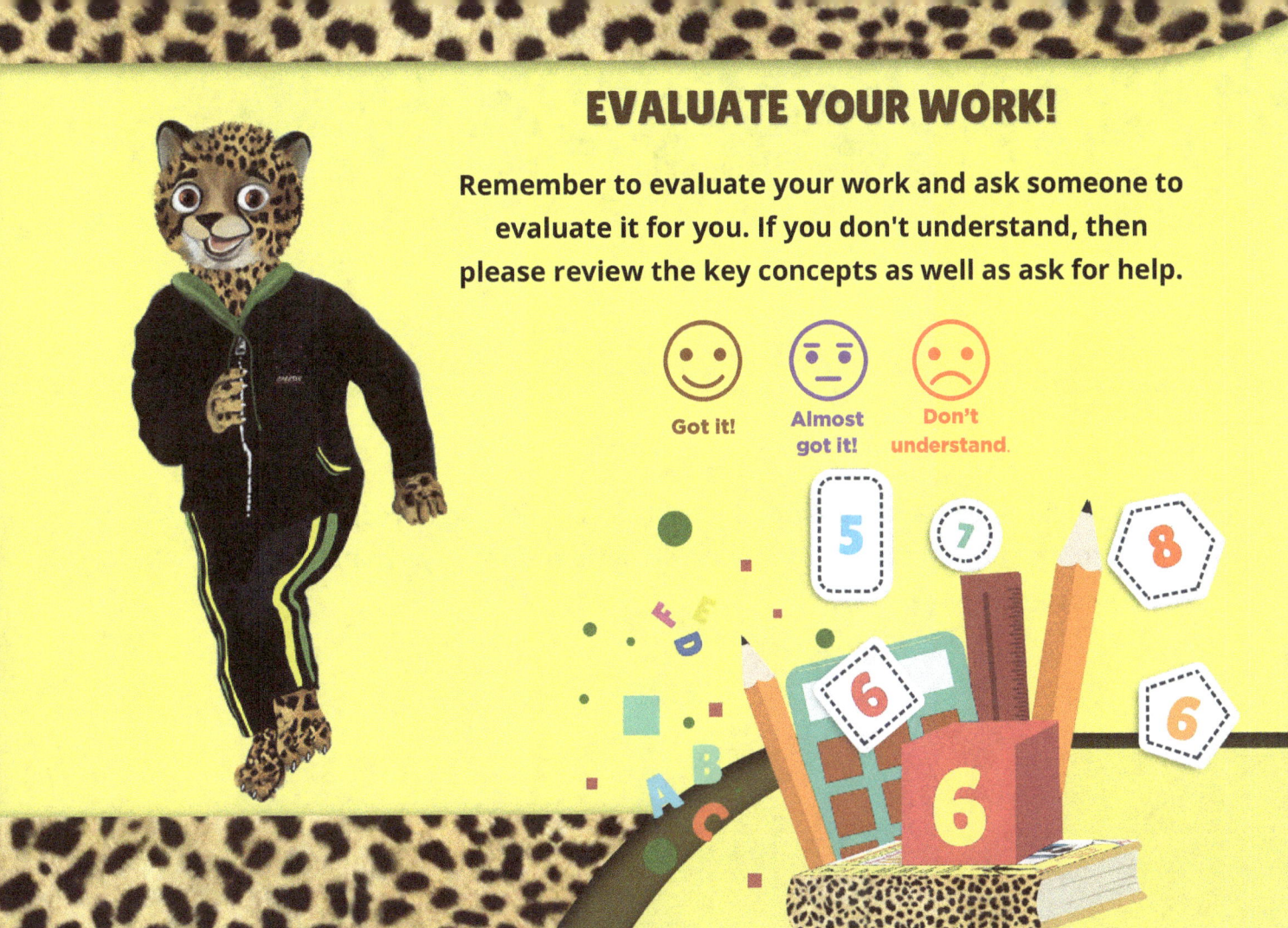

EVALUATE YOUR WORK!

Remember to evaluate your work and ask someone to evaluate it for you. If you don't understand, then please review the key concepts as well as ask for help.

- 🙂 Got it!
- 😐 Almost got it!
- ☹️ Don't understand.

My evaluation of the test: _____

What is my plan of action? What will I do next?

....
....
....
....
....
....

40-QUESTIONS TEST #8
ANSWER SHEET

The next page has an answer sheet that you will use to record your answers. It is similar to what you will most likely use during your PEP exams. Please remove this page.

(OPTIONAL HELPFUL INFORMATION)

TEST #: _____

START TIME: _____

END TIME: _____

SCORE: _____

Start this test whenever you are told to do so or whenever you are ready.

40-QUESTIONS TEST #8

Name: _____ ID no. _____ Age: ___

School: _____ School address: _____

1	Ⓐ	Ⓑ	Ⓒ	Ⓓ		21	Ⓐ	Ⓑ	Ⓒ	Ⓓ
2	Ⓐ	Ⓑ	Ⓒ	Ⓓ		22	Ⓐ	Ⓑ	Ⓒ	Ⓓ
3	Ⓐ	Ⓑ	Ⓒ	Ⓓ		23	Ⓐ	Ⓑ	Ⓒ	Ⓓ
4	Ⓐ	Ⓑ	Ⓒ	Ⓓ		24	Ⓐ	Ⓑ	Ⓒ	Ⓓ
5	Ⓐ	Ⓑ	Ⓒ	Ⓓ		25	Ⓐ	Ⓑ	Ⓒ	Ⓓ
6	Ⓐ	Ⓑ	Ⓒ	Ⓓ		26	Ⓐ	Ⓑ	Ⓒ	Ⓓ
7	Ⓐ	Ⓑ	Ⓒ	Ⓓ		27	Ⓐ	Ⓑ	Ⓒ	Ⓓ
8	Ⓐ	Ⓑ	Ⓒ	Ⓓ		28	Ⓐ	Ⓑ	Ⓒ	Ⓓ
9	Ⓐ	Ⓑ	Ⓒ	Ⓓ		29	Ⓐ	Ⓑ	Ⓒ	Ⓓ
10	Ⓐ	Ⓑ	Ⓒ	Ⓓ		30	Ⓐ	Ⓑ	Ⓒ	Ⓓ
11	Ⓐ	Ⓑ	Ⓒ	Ⓓ		31	Ⓐ	Ⓑ	Ⓒ	Ⓓ
12	Ⓐ	Ⓑ	Ⓒ	Ⓓ		32	Ⓐ	Ⓑ	Ⓒ	Ⓓ
13	Ⓐ	Ⓑ	Ⓒ	Ⓓ		33	Ⓐ	Ⓑ	Ⓒ	Ⓓ
14	Ⓐ	Ⓑ	Ⓒ	Ⓓ		34	Ⓐ	Ⓑ	Ⓒ	Ⓓ
15	Ⓐ	Ⓑ	Ⓒ	Ⓓ		35	Ⓐ	Ⓑ	Ⓒ	Ⓓ
16	Ⓐ	Ⓑ	Ⓒ	Ⓓ		36	Ⓐ	Ⓑ	Ⓒ	Ⓓ
17	Ⓐ	Ⓑ	Ⓒ	Ⓓ		37	Ⓐ	Ⓑ	Ⓒ	Ⓓ
18	Ⓐ	Ⓑ	Ⓒ	Ⓓ		38	Ⓐ	Ⓑ	Ⓒ	Ⓓ
19	Ⓐ	Ⓑ	Ⓒ	Ⓓ		39	Ⓐ	Ⓑ	Ⓒ	Ⓓ
20	Ⓐ	Ⓑ	Ⓒ	Ⓓ		40	Ⓐ	Ⓑ	Ⓒ	Ⓓ

Score _____ **out of 40**

www.mycheetahacademy.com

CHEETAH™ Toys & More, LLC Copyright 2022 © Copying is NOT allowed

CHEETAH™
Connect to **H**igher **E**ducation, **E**lectronic **T**ools, **A**plication and **H**elp

40-QUESTIONS TEST #8

1. Lloyd, Jamil, Joyce and Gilda walk to school every day. Lloyd leaves his house at 8.00 a.m. and arrives at school 25 minutes later. Jamil takes half the time to walk to school. Joyce is 5 minutes quicker than Lloyd, and Gilda's journey takes the longest. Which is the correct order of the children by time taken to walk to school, from shortest to longest?
   A. Lloyd, Jamil, Joyce, Gilda
   B. Jamil, Joyce, Lloyd, Gilda
   C. Joyce, Gilda, Lloyd, Jamil
   D. Gilda, Lloyd, Jamil, Joyce

The steps for building a home are shown in the pictures below.

1.

2.

3.

4.

5.

2. Which of the following sequences puts the steps of building a home into logical order?
   A. 5, 4, 2, 1, 3
   B. 4, 3, 1, 2, 5
   C. 4, 1, 3, 5, 2
   D. 3, 2, 4, 5, 1

The diagram below shows the favourite activities at a local nursery.

3. If 32 children like outdoor play the best, how many children prefer to play with water?

   A. 8　　　　　　　B. 6　　　　　　　C. 14　　　　　　　D. 10

4. Yesterday, I learnt to _____ the pain of a splinter in my finger.

   A. bear　　　　　　B. bair　　　　　　C. bare　　　　　　D. beer

The table below shows the daily average number of swimmers at a local beach over a four-year period. Use the information in the table to answer items 5 and 6.

	2017	2018	2019	2020
Men	60	50	80	55
Women	35	50	60	65
Children	70	60	50	70

5. Assuming that the children's group is 50% boys and 50% girls, which was the most popular year for males swimming at the beach?

A. 2017   B. 2018   C. 2019   D. 2020

6. How many more men swam at the beach over the four-year period when compared with women?

A. 30   B. 35   C. 40   D. 45

7. Alexa knows that the number of bacteria in her petri dish doubles every 20 minutes. She wants to predict how many bacteria will be in the petri dish after 2 hours. What information is necessary for her to reach a conclusion?

A. The number of bacteria in the petri dish at the start.
B. The size of one bacterium.
C. The size of the petri dish.
D. The temperature in the room.

In a survey, 100 Grade 6 students were asked which flavour of ice cream they like best.

- Most students prefer a fruit flavour.
- Chocolate ice cream was the least liked flavour.
- The same number of students like strawberry as those who like vanilla.

I.

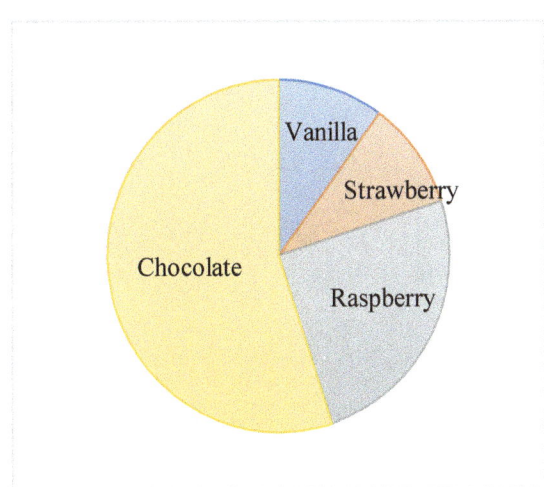

II.

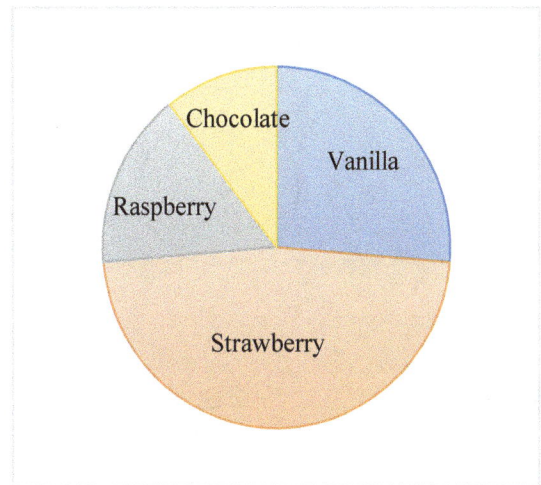

III.

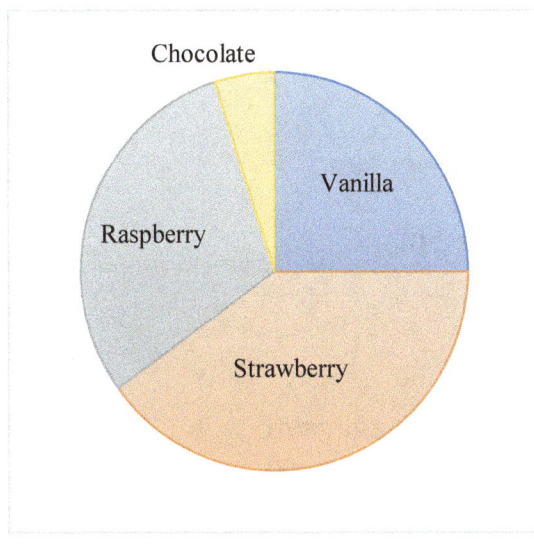

IV.

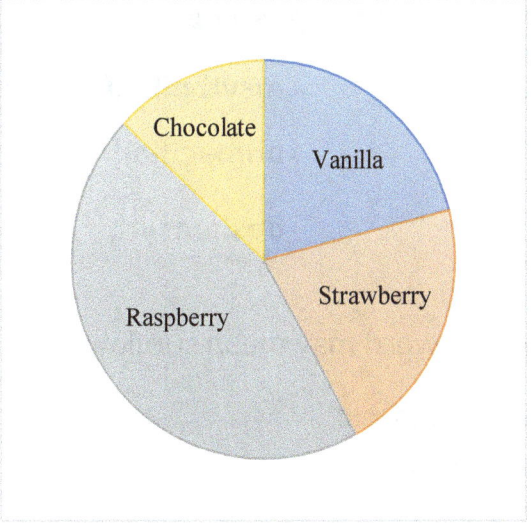

8. Which chart shows the information correctly?
- A. chart I
- B. chart II
- C. chart III
- D. chart IV

9. Look at the pattern shown below. Use the first two rows to work out the missing number in the third row.

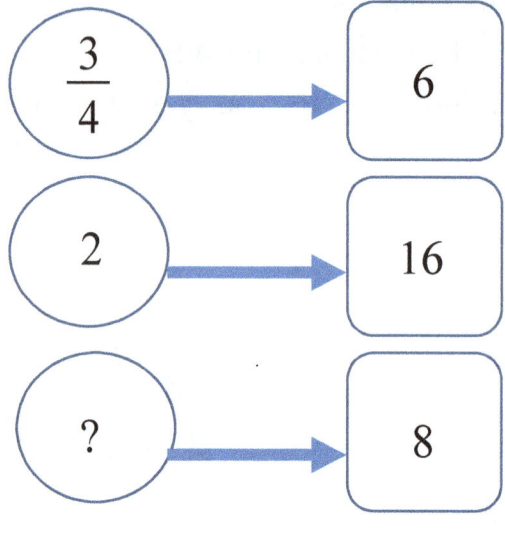

A. ¾　　　　　　B. 1　　　　　　C. 1½　　　　　　D. 7/8

Look at the words in bold. They are taken from an invented language. Next to each word is its English meaning.

msytbgihaif	means plant seed
ohmagihaif	means sunflower seed
baslpmsytb	means potted plant

10. Which word may mean sunflower plants?

   A. ohmabaslp　　　　　　　　C. ohmagimsytb
   B. gihaifmsytb　　　　　　　　D. baslpmhaif

For items 11 to 14, choose the word that best completes the sentence.

11. Hammer is to nail as _____ is to hair.
   A. long　　　　　　　　　　　C. brush
   B. curly　　　　　　　　　　　D. ponytail

12. Courage is to hero as _____ is to iguana.
    A. animal
    B. rodent
    C. scaly
    D. friendly

13. Happiness is to emotion as _____ is to fruit.
    A. vegetable
    B. food
    C. crunchy
    D. orange

14. Trembling is to fear as _____ is to amusement.
    A. laughing
    B. frowning
    C. anger
    D. riding

15. The teacher received a beautiful bunch of flowers. Half of the flowers were yellow. There were fewer pink flowers than orange flowers. A quarter of the flowers were red. Which of the following could **not** be the number of flowers in the bunch?
    A. 16
    B. 12
    C. 20
    D. 14

16. Each diagram below contains numbers that follow the same rule. Use the information in the first and second diagrams to work out the missing number in the third diagram.

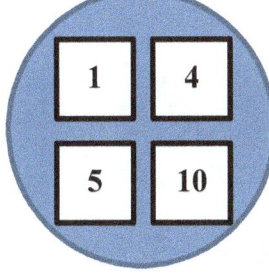 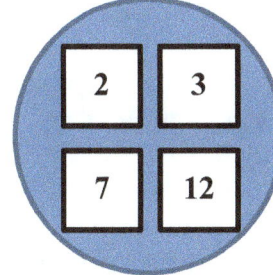 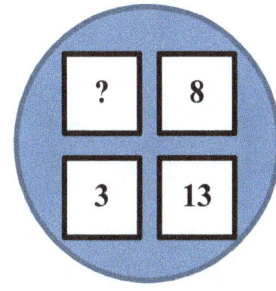

    A. 4
    B. 2
    C. 3
    D. 5

17. Bradley is the son of Clara. Adam and Clara are husband and wife. Edward is the brother of Clara. Dana is the daughter of Adam, and Freddie is her brother. Who is the uncle of Dana?
    A. Adam
    B. Bradley
    C. Freddie
    D. Edward

Read the passage below before answering questions 18 to 20.

The Bustamante Hospital for Children (BHC), located in Kingston, is the only **specialist** hospital for children in the entire English-speaking Caribbean. Previously a British military hospital, the site was given to the Jamaican government to mark Jamaica's Independence on November 6, 1962.

The **cutting-edge** care provided by the hospital is widely recognised and supported. As just one example, the Jamaican-American reggae singer and rapper, Shaggy, formed the Shaggy Make a Difference Foundation to raise funds for the hospital. The Shaggy and Friends Benefit Concert, featuring music stars from all around the world, is always a roaring success, raising millions of dollars for much-needed equipment.

In 2017, the hospital opened its own dedicated children's cardiac facility, thanks to the money raised by the hospital's supporters. In the past year, over 82 children suffering from various heart diseases have had their lives saved in that remarkable facility.

18. Which word means the same as 'cutting-edge'?
    A. advanced
    B. ancient
    C. aggressive
    D. useless

19. Which of the following facilities would also be considered 'specialist'?
    A. a supermarket
    B. a space-flight operations facility
    C. a car park
    D. a school canteen

20. Which of the following statements expresses the opinion of the writer?
    A. More celebrities should support the hospital.
    B. There are better ways to raise money than by staging a concert.
    C. The facilities at the hospital need to be improved.
    D. The hospital's department for treating heart disease is very impressive.

Look at the number in the circle shown. Multiply by 5.

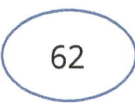

21. What is the place value of the digit '0' in the answer?
    A. tens
    B. thousands
    C. hundreds
    D. ones

Below is a diagram of an L-shaped hexagon (**LMNOPQ**).

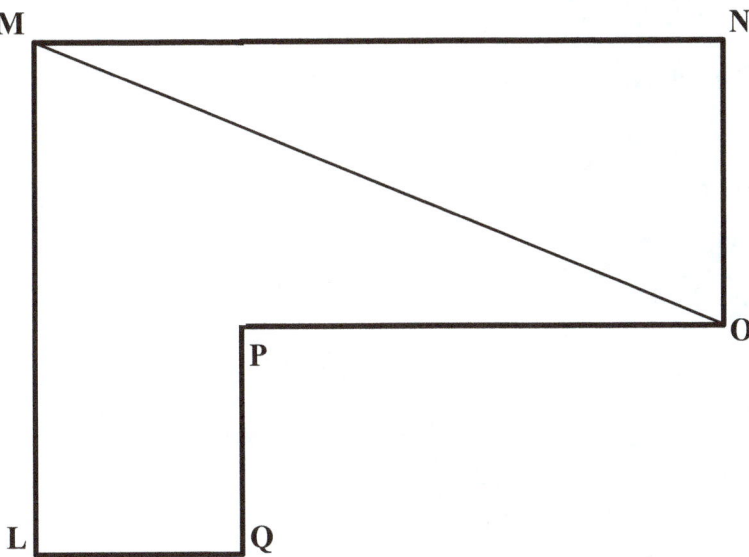

22. The shortest length is shown by which of the following?
    A. ML + NO
    B. MO + LQ
    C. LQ + NO
    D. NO + PQ

Use the pattern shown to answer this question.

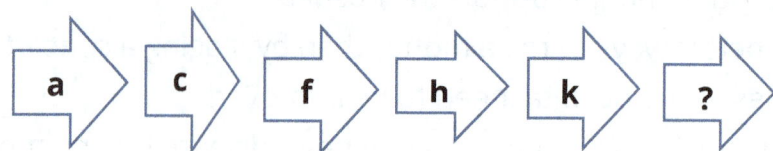

23. What is the next letter in the chain?

A. m B. l C. n D. o

The diagram below shows the location of Noel in the town centre.

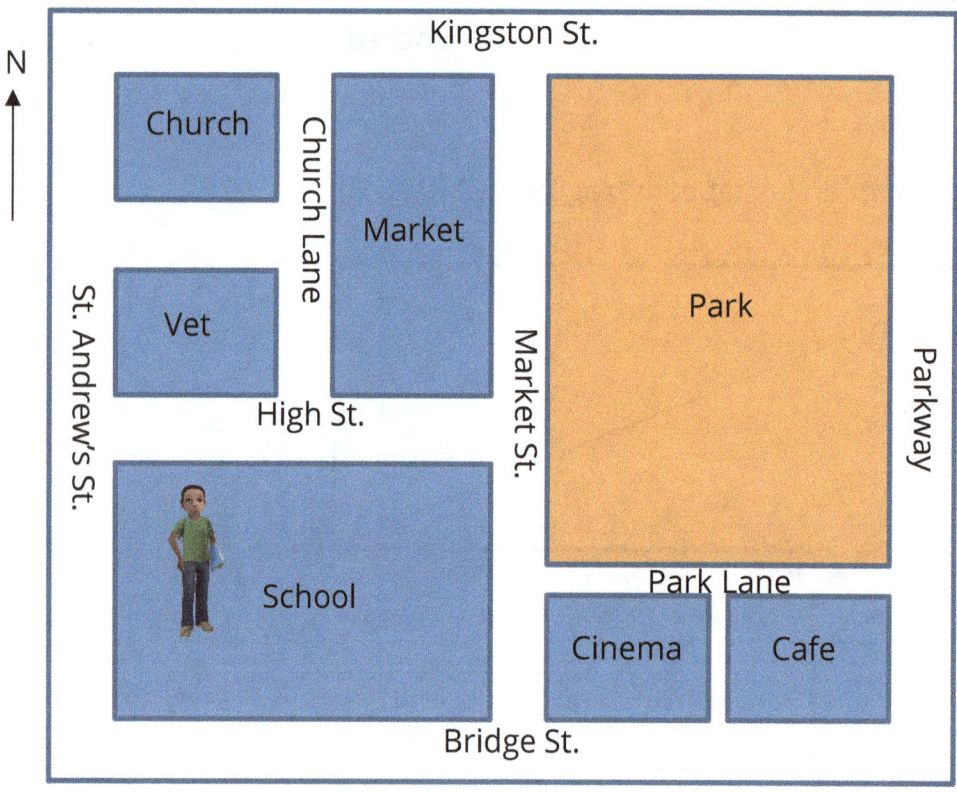

24. Using the information given, which of the following statements is correct?

A. If Noel heads north on St Andrew's Street and east on Kingston Street, he will reach the cinema.

B. The Market is southeast from where Noel is standing.

C. If Noel heads north on St Andrew's Street and east on High Street, he will reach the park.

D. St. Andrew's Street and Kingston Street run parallel to one another.

40-QUESTIONS TEST #8

25. Peter is sorting shapes. He discovers that some of the shapes are rectangles while others are triangles. When he counts all the sides of the shapes, he determines that they have 11 sides in total. Which of the numbers below is the total number of **triangles**?

    A. 1 B. 2 C. 3 D. 4

For items 26 to 28, choose the word that does not fit the group.

26. A. lizard C. manatee
    B. turtle D. shark

27. A. rob C. donate
    B. thieve D. steal

28. A. repair C. hammer
    B. mend D. fix

29. At a school fair, attendees were asked to estimate the number of sweets in a jar. Whoever guessed closest to the actual amount of 789 sweets would be the winner and take home the sweets! Which of the following guesses won the sweets in the jar?

    A. 785 B. 783 C. 794 D. 792

For items 30 to 32, choose the best word to complete each statement.

30. It was time for the farmer to _____ the field.
    A. plow C. plowe
    B. plough D. plaugh

31. The business needed to _____ more staff.
    A. annoy C. employ
    B. envoy D. enjoy

32. The market is extremely busy, always _____ with people.
    A. barren C. swarming
    B. dealing D. sparse

33. A tour bus has a staff of 3 people and can carry a total of 18 people at any one time. How many buses will be needed to carry 100 tourists from the Sangster International Airport to their hotels?

A. 4 B. 5 C. 6 D. 7

34. Circle the most suitable answer.

 is to  as  is to...

A.

C.

B.

D.

40-QUESTIONS TEST #8

Below are two boxes, each containing an extract. Read the texts, then complete items 35 and 36.

Extract 1

Jamaica formed its first football club in 1893, and the sport has grown in popularity ever since. The Jamaican Football Federation organises a National Premier League, as well as international men's and women's teams.

The international men's football team, the 'Reggae Boyz,' are going from strength to strength! In 1998, they finished third in the Final Round Qualifying for the FIFA World Cup, and in 2015 and 2017, the team reached the finals of the Concacaf Gold Cup.

Extract 2

In Jamaica, playing cricket predates 1895, when the Jamaican Scorpions (the national team) had three matches against a touring English team.

Today, Jamaica rarely competes in international competitions, and has won the domestic first-class competition eight times. The best Jamaican players are selected for the West Indies cricket team, an international representation of many countries in the Caribbean region.

35. Based on the information presented in the extracts, select the most appropriate answer.
    A. Jamaicans have been playing football for longer than they have been playing cricket.
    B. The Jamaican Football Federation organises national and international football matches, while the Jamaican Scorpions organises national and international cricket matches.
    C. Jamaica has a football team that plays international matches but does not have a cricket team that plays international matches.
    D. All of the above statements are false.

36. In what year did the Reggae Boys first reach the finals of the Concacaf Gold Cup.
    A. 1998
    B. 2015
    C. 1895
    D. 2005

40-QUESTIONS TEST #8

37. Look closely at the words in the box, then choose the logical sequence.

> leopard   animal
> mammal
> cat

   A. animal, cat, leopard, mammal
   B. mammal, animal, cat, leopard
   C. cat, leopard, animal, mammal
   D. leopard, cat, mammal, animal

38. Choose the number that completes the following sequence:

3 | 9 | 27 | ? | 243

   A. 60
   B. 54
   C. 81
   D. 72

For items 39 and 40, choose the word that is an essential part of the word in capital letters.

39. SWIMMING
   A. swimming costume
   B. ocean
   C. towel
   D. water

40. FOREST
   A. grass
   B. wildlife
   C. trees
   D. leaves

CHEETAH® CHALLENGE

Before we end our preparation sessions, I would like you to review the key concepts at the beginning of this workbook. Do you understand the major categories of questions that you may be asked to answer?

Regardless of your response:

1. review the key concepts again
2. explain them to someone else (a peer, parent/guardian, or even a teacher)
3. with a peer, create a chart with all the various question types for **Test # 8**, **questions 1 to 10.** Try to put each question into one or more of the categories. Your chart should look similar to the one below, and I have completed question 1 for you.

Each question will be less challenging if you FIRST understand what is expected of you.

Q	Verbal Reasoning	Non-Verbal Reasoning	Numeracy	Quantitative Reasoning	Abstract Reasoning	Analytical Reasoning	Logical Reasoning
1.	✓		✓	✓		✓	
2.							
3.							
4.							
5.							
6.							
7.							
8.							
9.							
10.							

Add more questions if you are feeling adventurous.

Will you accept my CHEETAH® CHALLENGE?

Do not be afraid to ask for help!

EVALUATE YOUR WORK!

Remember to evaluate your work and ask someone to evaluate it for you. If you don't understand, then please review the key concepts as well as ask for help.

Got it!   Almost got it!   Don't understand.

My evaluation of the test:_____

What is my plan of action? What will I do next?

....
....
....
....
....
....
....

40-QUESTIONS TEST #8

How did you do? Did you finish all the questions within the 1 hour and 30 minutes? Share your results with your teacher and discuss the wrong answers.

Remember that "The only place where success comes before work is in the dictionary." **Vidal Sassoon**

40-QUESTIONS TEST #9
ANSWER SHEET

The next page has an answer sheet that you will use to record your answers. It is similar to what you will most likely use during your PEP exams. Please remove this page.

(OPTIONAL HELPFUL INFORMATION)

TEST #: _____

START TIME: _____

END TIME: _____

SCORE: _____

Start this test whenever you are told to do so or whenever you are ready.

40-QUESTIONS TEST #9

Name: _____ ID no. _____ Age: ____

School: _____ School address: _____

1	Ⓐ	Ⓑ	Ⓒ	Ⓓ	21	Ⓐ	Ⓑ	Ⓒ	Ⓓ
2	Ⓐ	Ⓑ	Ⓒ	Ⓓ	22	Ⓐ	Ⓑ	Ⓒ	Ⓓ
3	Ⓐ	Ⓑ	Ⓒ	Ⓓ	23	Ⓐ	Ⓑ	Ⓒ	Ⓓ
4	Ⓐ	Ⓑ	Ⓒ	Ⓓ	24	Ⓐ	Ⓑ	Ⓒ	Ⓓ
5	Ⓐ	Ⓑ	Ⓒ	Ⓓ	25	Ⓐ	Ⓑ	Ⓒ	Ⓓ
6	Ⓐ	Ⓑ	Ⓒ	Ⓓ	26	Ⓐ	Ⓑ	Ⓒ	Ⓓ
7	Ⓐ	Ⓑ	Ⓒ	Ⓓ	27	Ⓐ	Ⓑ	Ⓒ	Ⓓ
8	Ⓐ	Ⓑ	Ⓒ	Ⓓ	28	Ⓐ	Ⓑ	Ⓒ	Ⓓ
9	Ⓐ	Ⓑ	Ⓒ	Ⓓ	29	Ⓐ	Ⓑ	Ⓒ	Ⓓ
10	Ⓐ	Ⓑ	Ⓒ	Ⓓ	30	Ⓐ	Ⓑ	Ⓒ	Ⓓ
11	Ⓐ	Ⓑ	Ⓒ	Ⓓ	31	Ⓐ	Ⓑ	Ⓒ	Ⓓ
12	Ⓐ	Ⓑ	Ⓒ	Ⓓ	32	Ⓐ	Ⓑ	Ⓒ	Ⓓ
13	Ⓐ	Ⓑ	Ⓒ	Ⓓ	33	Ⓐ	Ⓑ	Ⓒ	Ⓓ
14	Ⓐ	Ⓑ	Ⓒ	Ⓓ	34	Ⓐ	Ⓑ	Ⓒ	Ⓓ
15	Ⓐ	Ⓑ	Ⓒ	Ⓓ	35	Ⓐ	Ⓑ	Ⓒ	Ⓓ
16	Ⓐ	Ⓑ	Ⓒ	Ⓓ	36	Ⓐ	Ⓑ	Ⓒ	Ⓓ
17	Ⓐ	Ⓑ	Ⓒ	Ⓓ	37	Ⓐ	Ⓑ	Ⓒ	Ⓓ
18	Ⓐ	Ⓑ	Ⓒ	Ⓓ	38	Ⓐ	Ⓑ	Ⓒ	Ⓓ
19	Ⓐ	Ⓑ	Ⓒ	Ⓓ	39	Ⓐ	Ⓑ	Ⓒ	Ⓓ
20	Ⓐ	Ⓑ	Ⓒ	Ⓓ	40	Ⓐ	Ⓑ	Ⓒ	Ⓓ

Score _____ out of 40

www.mycheetahacademy.com

CHEETAH™ Toys & More, LLC Copyright 2022 © Copying is NOT allowed

Connect to Higher Education, Electronic Tools, Aplication and Help

40-QUESTIONS TEST #9

1. What is the missing number?

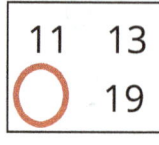

   A. 14   B. 15   C. 17   D. 18

2. Choose the sentence with the CORRECT spelling:
   A. I received a reciept from Hi Lo Supermarket yesterday.
   B. The price of the oranges was incorrect on the receipt.
   C. I filed the receit away in case I needed to check it later.
   D. 'Please don't forget your risseete!' called the shop assistant.

3. Which is the next number in the following sequence: 3, 4, 5, 7, 9, 12, 15?
   A. 19   B. 18   C. 22   D. 17

4. In 7 years, the sum of the ages of my sister and her 3 children will be 92. What will it be in 4 years?
   A. 80   B. 84   C. 96   D. 108

5. What fraction is represented by the dot on the number line?

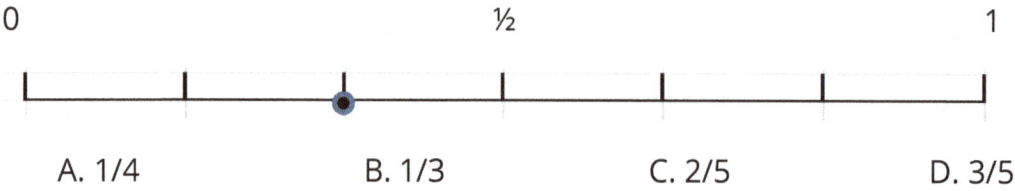

   A. 1/4   B. 1/3   C. 2/5   D. 3/5

Maria is older than Tommy. Johnny is older than Maria. Tommy is older than Johnny.

6. If the first two sentences are true, the third one is
   A. true   C. uncertain
   B. false   D. partly true

40-QUESTIONS TEST #9

7. Examine the steps below and use the information to identify the correct sequence.
   I. sit test
   II. gather notes
   III. know what the test is about
   IV. study and practise

   A. II, III, IV, I
   B. III IV, I II
   C. III, II, IV, I
   D. II, IV, I, III

8. There is an equal number of red, blue, and yellow towels in your aunt's suitcase. How many towels could be in the suitcase?
   A. 16
   B. 29
   C. 37
   D. 42

9. In order to get to school each day, I have to take a JUTC Bus and a taxi. If the bus takes 23 minutes, and my time spent in the taxi is 49 minutes, how much time do I spend travelling each day?
   A. 2 hours and 24 minutes
   B. 2 hours and 35 minutes
   C. 72 minutes
   D. 85 minutes

Look at the family tree below and answer items 10 and 11.

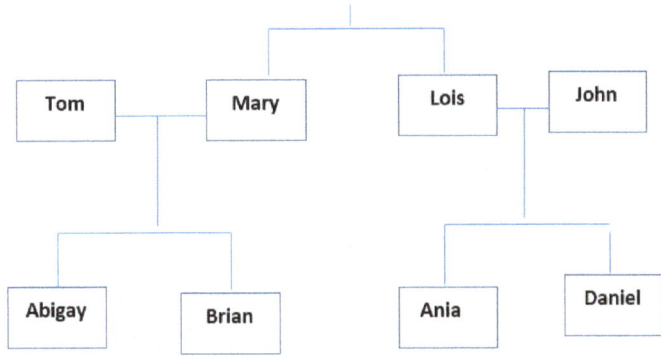

10. What is the relationship between Abigay and John?
    A. daughter and father
    B. first cousins
    C. siblings
    D. niece and uncle

11. What is the relationship between Brian and Daniel?
   A. uncle and nephew
   B. first cousins
   C. siblings
   D. father and son

12. A carpenter wants to cut a 10-metre plank into 10 equal parts. If he takes 1 minute per cut, how long does it take him?
   A. 11 minutes
   B. 10 minutes
   C. 9 minutes
   D. 8 minutes

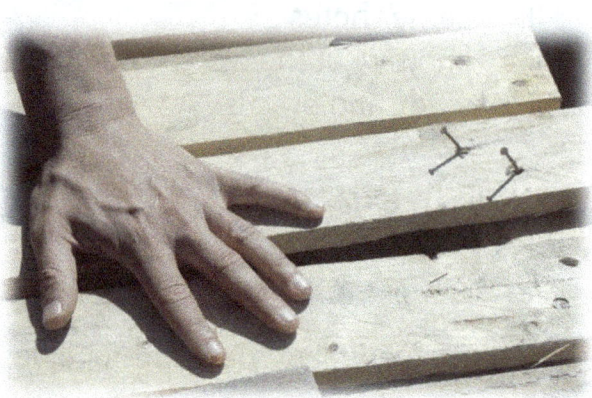

13. Ring is to rang as go is to _____.
   A. gone
   B. went
   C. did
   D. let

14. Find the next number in this series:
   15, 14, 12, 9, _____
   A. 3
   B. 4
   C. 7
   D. 5

15. Find the next number in this series:
   4, 3 ½, 3, 2 ½, _____
   A. 1 ½
   B. ½
   C. 2
   D. 1

16. The day after tomorrow is four days before Monday. What day is today?
   A. Monday
   B. Tuesday
   C. Wednesday
   D. Friday

17. Well is to sick as present is to _____.
   A. decline
   B. absent
   C. future
   D. away

40-QUESTIONS TEST #9

18. A man walks 2 km east, then he turns and walks 4 km south. Next, he turns and walks 6 km west, before turning and walking 4 km north. How far is the man from his starting point?

   A. 2 km B. 3 km C. 4 km D. 6 km

19. Using the letters in the alphabet, what is the next pair of letters in the series?

   A, B, C, D, E, F, G, H, I, J, K, L, M, N, O, P, Q, R, S, T, U, V, W, X, Y, Z

   Sequence: BY, DW, FU, HS, __.
   A. JQ B. CX C. HQ D. LM

20. A sightseeing tour requires a staff of 2 people, and the helicopter can carry a total of 8 people at any one time. How many helicopter tours will be needed to transport 50 tourists?

   A. 7 B. 6 C. 9 D. 8

21. Fill in the blanks to form one word that is an antonym of the word 'poverty'.

	E				H

   What is the word?
   A. hearth B. health C. wealth D. detach

22. Which of the following words is a necessary component of a library?
   A. shelves B. people C. books D. windows

For items 23 to 25, select the set of words which is the odd one out.

23. A. tree – trunk   C. coat – sleeve
    B. house – room   D. wall – fence

24. A. hot – cold   C. new – old
    B. late – early   D. push – shove

25. A. blue – blew   C. cell – sell
    B. here – hear   D. light - fight

26. Divide the product of 20 and 12 by their difference.
   A. 20
   B. 8
   C. 30
   D. 16

27. What time should the fifth watch show?

   A. 4:13   B. 4:25   C. 4:30   D. 4:45

28. At a school tuck shop, a small book costs $50, a pen costs $30, a pencil costs $25 and a sharpener costs $25. If a student spends $290 at the tuck shop, which combination of items could have been purchased for exactly that amount?
   A. 2 books, 2 pens, 4 pencils and 1 sharpener
   B. 2 books, 3 pens, 3 pencils and 1 sharpener
   C. 1 book, 3 pens, 8 pencils and 4 sharpeners
   D. 2 books, 2 pens, 3 pencils and 2 sharpeners

29. Edward is the son of Amanda. Daniel is the son of Bill. Edward is married to Cecilia. Cecilia is Bill's daughter. How is Daniel related to Cecilia?
   A. Daniel is Cecilia's husband.
   B. Daniel is Cecilia's father.
   C. Daniel is Cecilia's brother.
   D. Daniel is Cecilia's uncle.

30. Look closely at the words in the bubble, then choose the logical sequence.
   A. knee, heel, face, chest
   B. face, chest, heel, knee
   C. chest, knee, face, heel
   D. heel, knee, chest, face

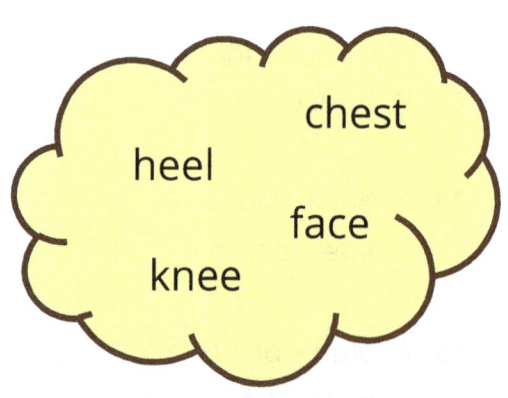

40–QUESTIONS TEST #9

For items 31 and 32, choose the BEST word for the blank space.

31. Calm is to peaceful as dirty is to _____
    A. filthy
    B. used
    C. old
    D. clean

32. Boat is to goat as escape is to _____
    A. cow
    B. fast
    C. tape
    D. run

Below are two boxes, each containing an extract. Read the texts, then decide whether the conclusions reached in item 33 are true, false, partially true or unable to tell.

Extract 1

A Bob Marley Nine Mile tour is an absolute must for reggae fans! Nine Mile is a sleepy Jamaican town, high in the mountains, and both the birthplace and the resting place of this famous musician.

Marley's mausoleum is a celebration of his life, and contains many of the legendary singer's guitars, awards and photographs. A Rasta-coloured 'rock pillow' is also nearby, which Marley is said to have laid his head on when seeking inspiration.

Extract 2

Elvis Presley, born in Tupelo, Mississippi, was an American singer widely known as the 'King of Rock and Roll.' His mansion home in Memphis, Tennessee, named 'Graceland,' is now a tourist attraction visited by more than 600,000 fans per year.

Graceland is also the world-famous singer's final resting place. While first interred in a public cemetery in Memphis, an attempt to tamper with the grave resulted in Elvis being moved to the Meditation Garden at his home.

33. More fans visit Graceland each year than the number of fans who visit Nine Mile.
    A. true
    B. false
    C. partially true
    D. unable to tell

34. Which of the following words does not belong to the group?
    A. duckling
    B. foal
    C. cub
    D. lion

35. Look at the group of words in the bubble. Which of the following words completes the group?
   A. leaf
   C. petal
   B. dirt
   D. grass

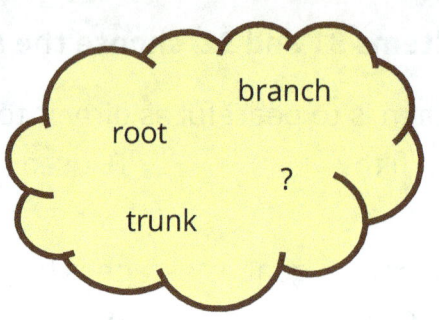

36. Abe is 180 cm tall, which is 3 times the height of his daughter, Sheree. Sheree is 18 cm shorter than her brother, Michael. How tall is Michael?
   A. 60 cm
   B. 42 cm
   C. 70 cm
   D. 78 cm

37. In a row of houses, a house is 8th from the left end and 21st from the right end. How many houses are in the row?
   A. 29
   B. 27
   C. 28
   D. 30

38. BALL is written in a number code as 1233. WHALE is written in the same code as 45236. Using this code, what number will represent the first letter in the word HOUSE?
   A. 7
   B. 5
   C. 2
   D. 4

39. Which of the following nets will make the cube shown below?

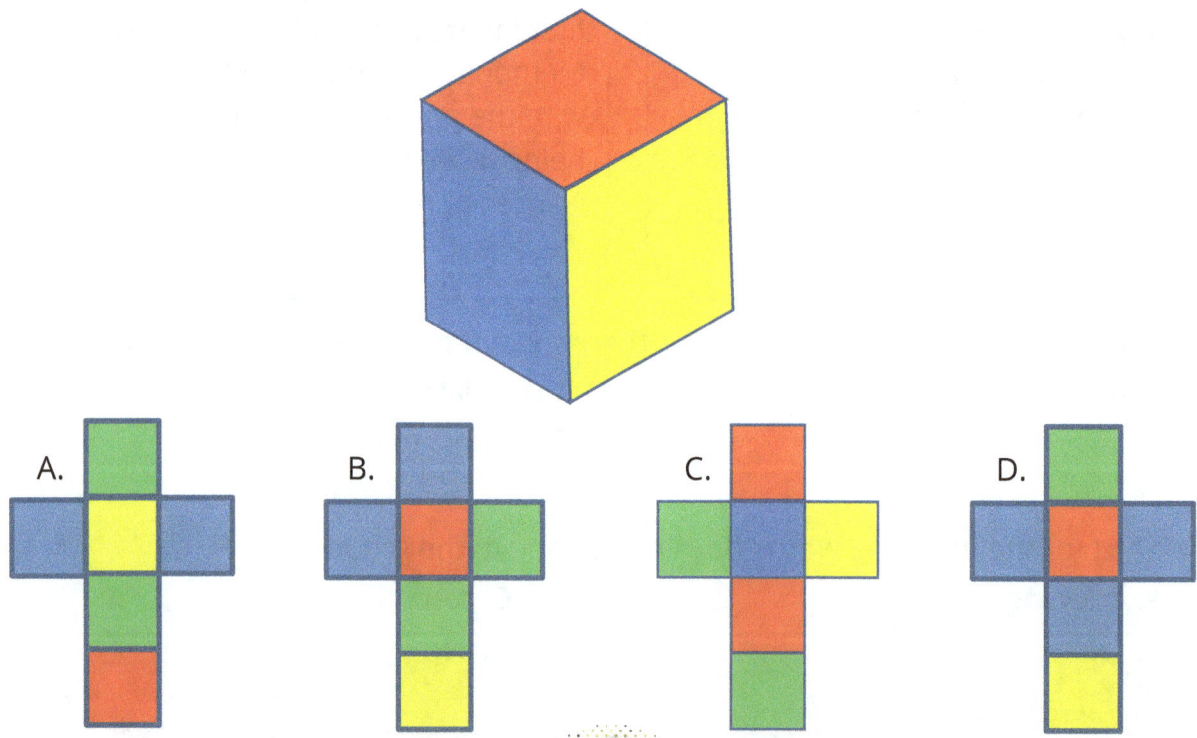

40-QUESTIONS TEST #9

Use the clues below to answer the following question.

The second digit is 6.

He has no more than $300.

The third digit is the product of 2 and 4.

40. How much money does Jevaughn have in his pocket?
    A. $368
    B. $160
    C. $268
    D. $286

According to Bob Marley, 'True friends are like stars; you only recognize them when it's dark around you.'

Do you agree? Hoping these test questions are not making your world 'dark'. Hoping you have stars in your corner.

Come wid mi. Mek wi continue!

EVALUATE YOUR WORK!

Remember to evaluate your work and ask someone to evaluate it for you. If you don't understand, then please review the key concepts as well as ask for help.

Got it!   Almost got it!   Don't understand.

My evaluation of the test:_____

What is my plan of action? What will I do next?

....
....
....
....
....
....

Answers and explanations

Are you ready for the answers and explanations?

Remember our honour system.

Do not review this section until after you have completed the questions.

40-QUESTIONS TEST #1

Answer key

Question	Answer	Explanation
1.	B. night	While light is a product of the sun being in the sky in the day, dark is a product of the sun no longer being in the sky, at night.
2.	C. goat	While piglets are young pigs, kids are young goats.
3.	D. small	While the opposite of wet is dry, the opposite of big is small.
4.	A. empty	While the opposite of soft is hard, the opposite of full is empty.
5.	D. pages	A book may include words, pictures or a blurb, but it always contain pages. This makes pages essential for a book.
6.	B. sound	Music may feature drums, singing, or guitar, but without sound there is no music.
7.	D. iguana	Owl, cuckoo and pigeon are all types of birds, while iguana is a type of lizard.
8.	A. dominoes	Cricket, athletics and football are all games that require the movement of the entire body, whereas dominoes is a board game and only requires the movement of the hands.

ANSWERS AND EXPLANATIONS: 40-QUESTIONS TEST #2

Question	Answer	Explanation
9.	C. school	Teachers, students and parents are all groups of people associated with a school, whereas 'school' is the building itself.
10.	D. sometimes	If something happens 'now and again', it happens occasionally or sometimes, but not all the time.
11.	C. long tail hummingbird	An endangered species is an animal or plant at risk of having no living members. Sheep, rats and cats are plentiful, however the long tail hummingbird (doctor bird) is an endangered specie.
12.	A. to inform the reader about Jamaican Boas	The passage describes the Jamaican Boa.
13.	D. 3, 5, 1, 4, 2	The raw ingredients feature in image 3, which are mixed together in image 5. Once the ingredients are mixed, they can be rolled as in image 1. Image 4 shows the rolled circles being fried in a pan, while image 2 is of the final, cooked roti presented ready to serve.
14.	A. frog	An egg develops into a tadpole. A tadpole develops into a froglet, which then develops into a frog.
15.	B. tree, wood, paper, book	A tree must be cut down to gather wood. Wood can then be used to make

ANSWERS AND EXPLANATIONS: 40-QUESTIONS TEST #2

Question	Answer	Explanation
		paper, which is then used to make a book.
16.	B. false	If the first two are true, then Tommy is the youngest. Therefore, the third sentence must be false.
17.	C. exercise	Exercise is a physical activity requiring effort, which strengthens muscles and bones.
18.	B. surrounded	To be considered an island, a piece of land MUST be surrounded by water.
19.	D. buy	This spelling of the word means to obtain the eggs in exchange for payment.
20.	A. true	If 'the national flag of Jamaica is the only flag in the world that has no colours in common with the U.S. flag', then every other flag shares a colour with the U.S. flag, including the flag of Mauritania.
21.	C. unable to tell	The text tells us that much of Mauritania is desert. We are told nothing of the vegetation in the south of the country where there is rain. 'Unable to tell' is therefore the correct option.
22.	B. 56	The rule of the sequence is +5, +10. As the previous two numbers are 41 and

ANSWERS AND EXPLANATIONS: 40-QUESTIONS TEST #2

Question	Answer	EXPLANATION
		46, their difference of 5 tells us that the next number will be 46+10, which is 56.
23.	B. 61	Subtracting the bottom right-hand number from the bottom left-hand number will give you the top number in the triangle, so, 69-8=61.
24.	B. 9	In each case, multiply the numbers on each side by 3.
25.	A. chart I	There are 4 heart shapes, 7 triangles and 2 circles.
26.	D. chart IV	Throwing and jumping have equal sized segments, while the sector representing running is more than half of the circle.
27.	B.	One third of the rectangle is shaded, which is the same as the circular segment which is also one third. If two-thirds of the rectangle is shaded, it will be the same as a segment which is two-thirds of a circle.
28.	D. Victoria, Joshua, Dominic, Raheem	It is stated that Raheem is the oldest. Dominic is twice as old as Joshua, making him the second oldest, as Joshua is 2 years older than Victoria, who must be the youngest.
29.	B. 11	There cannot be 11 yellow bananas because there were only 10 on the bunch in the first place.

ANSWERS AND EXPLANATIONS: 40–QUESTIONS TEST #2

Question	Answer	Explanation
30.	D. It is impossible to determine the result based on the information given.	It would depend on the number Roseanne chose. For example, choosing the number 1 would make the column A result lower than the column B result. Choosing number 2, on the other hand, would give the same result for both columns. If she chose numbers 3 to 10, the column A result would be greater than that on column B.
31.	A. EF + FG	The longest length is the diagonal (FG), followed by the longer sides of the rectangle (EF and GH).
32.	D. 25,789	25,789 would round **up** to 26,000 people, not 25,000.
33.	C. 15 and 16	Odd-numbered pages will always be on the left-hand side, and even-numbered pages on the right.
34.	D. the length of the side of the garden and the length of the bricks	If Crystal knows the length of the side of the garden, she can divide this distance by the length of the brick to calculate how many bricks she will need altogether.
35.	A. day 1	Adding up the total sales for each day, 15 units were sold on day 1, compared to 38 units and 48 units on days 2 and 3 respectively.
36.	C. $3.00	On day 3 the unit price of chocolate chip icecream was $20/10 = $2.

ANSWERS AND EXPLANATIONS: 40-QUESTIONS TEST #2

Question	Answer	Explanation
		However, before the change, the unit price for day 2 was $6/2 =$3.
37.	A. 8 hours	The sleeping sector is one eighth of the chart. Football is represented by half of the chart, or four-eighths, so 4 x 2 hours is 8 hours playing football.
38.	C. 6	The crew of 6 people will be present for every flight, meaning that 14 passengers can be transported each time. 14 passengers x 6 flights = 84 passengers transported in total. Hence 6 flights are needed to transport up to 80 passengers.
39.	D. The hours of sunshine in Region B steadily decreased.	The line for Region B has no fluctuations, starting at a higher point in January and decreasing by approximately the same number of hours each month.
40.	A. 60	If half of the fish are snappers, a quarter must be herring and another quarter soldier fish for there to be equal amounts of each. The total number of fish in the net must therefore be divisible by 4.

40-QUESTIONS TEST #2

Answer key

Question	Answer	Explanation
1.	D. 247	Each large square is 10 cubes by 10 cubes, and 10x10=100. There are 2 of those, so that's 200 altogether. Each stick has 10 cubes, and there are 4 of them: 10x4=40. Then there are 7 individual cubes. 200 + 40 + 7 = 247.
2.	C. alarm	Alarm warns us of danger.
3.	D. lioness	A lioness is the female lion.
4.	B. dress	Each word in the sequence is used to make what comes next: yarn can be made from cotton, fabric can be made from yarn, and a dress can be made from a piece of fabric.
5.	D. 21	We subtract 3 – 1 = 2 6 – 3 = 3 10 – 6 = 4 15 – 10 = 5 So, you will notice that we add the numbers 2, 3, 4, 5... to get the next number in the sequence. So, the missing answer is 15 + 6 = 21.

ANSWERS AND EXPLANATIONS: 40-QUESTIONS TEST #2

Question	Answer	Explanation
6.	C. 9	The number at the centre of each triangle equals the sum of the lower two numbers minus the top number. First triangle: 7 + 9 − 4 = 12 Answer triangle: 6 + 5 − 2 = 9
7.	B. take off	**T**ake-off means to fly.
8.	A. take down	Take down means to write down.
9.	D. certain	If all the marbles are blue, then you are certain to pull out a blue one.
10.	A. 6	Perimeter = base + base + side + side 20 = b + b + 4 + 4 20 = 2b + 8 20 − 8 = 2b 12 = 2b 2b = 12 b = 12/2 b = 6
11.	A. lightning	The light that comes from the clouds is called lightning.
12.	B. take off	Take off means to undress or remove.
13.	D. protein	Proteins are the nutrients in foods that build our muscles.

www.mycheetahacademy.com

CHEETAH™ Toys & More, LLC Copyright 2022 © Copying is NOT allowed

Question	Answer	Explanation
14.	B. 39 metres	The distance = 13 m x 3 = 39 m
15.	A. 4, 1, 2, 3	 **The cycle of a butterfly has four stages, starting with:** (4) Caterpillar eggs laid by a female butterfly. (1) The caterpillar leaves its egg and goes to the outside world. (2) The pupa is a fully grown caterpillar which has turned itself into a kind of vessel. (3) The butterfly, which is grown in the pupa, emerges.
16.	D. 3	The maximum number of hot dogs he can buy = 6/2 = 3 hot dogs.
17.	B. keyboard	A necessary component is something that has to be there. A computer works with a keyboard. All the other options are not parts of a computer.
18.	C. board	Every classroom has a board. The other items are not always in a classroom.
19.	D. 2500	The total number of passengers is 310 x 8 = 2,480. When rounded off 2480 is about 2,500.

ANSWERS AND EXPLANATIONS: 40–QUESTIONS TEST #2

Question	Answer	Explanation
20.	A. 0	The number in the biggest circle is the difference between the two small circles. First shape: 3 - 2 = 1 Second shape: 9 – 6 = 3 The answer: 5 – 5 = 0
21.	C. 545	The first digit is half of 10, 10/2=5. The second digit is 7 - 3=4. The final digit is an odd number, making the only possible answer 545.
22.	B. 10 minutes	The period of each problem = the whole time divided by the number of questions. 180 / 18= 10 minutes
23.	C. GK	Begin at letter A and N, move 2 letters to the right from A and 1 letter to the left from N: CM Repeat that process. Begin at C and M. Move 2 letters to the right from C and 1 letter to the left from M. OR The letters represent the numbers below them. Adding them together, AN = 1+14 = 15, CM = 3+13 = 16, EL = 5+12 = 17. The next pair of letters must therefore add to a total of 18, with the first letter representing the number 7. G =7 and K = 11, which totals 18.

ANSWERS AND EXPLANATIONS: 40-QUESTIONS TEST #2

Question	Answer	Explanation
24.	D. April	A, B and C are days of the week, but D is a month of the year.
25.	D. wood	Answers A, B and C are all forms of water (as a liquid, solid and gas respectively), but answer D is not a form of water.
26.	B. the green arrow	Since 6/8 is less than one whole, it must lie between 0 and 1 on the number line. It is equivalent to 3/4, so it is bigger than ½. The most suitable option is the green arrow that is closer to 1 rather than 0.
27.	A. week 1	In week 1 only 10 dishes of jerked chicken were sold, compared to 17 dishes in week 2 and 20 in week 3.
28.	C. stewed peas	Adding together the total sales across the 3 weeks: Ackee and saltfish: 15+10+10 = 35 dishes sold. Jerked chicken: 10+17+20 = 47 dishes sold. Stewed peas: 7+30+45 = 82 dishes sold
29.	B. false	Anything 'domestic' relates to the home and family. As they 'live in the jungle', 'don't depend on humans' and can 'hurt or eat humans', we can conclude that wild animals are not domestic.
30.	B. false	Rabbits are pets and part of the lives of many children. We love to 'groom and feed' pets and 'they are friendly and cute'. We can

ANSWERS AND EXPLANATIONS: 40-QUESTIONS TEST #2

Question	Answer	Explanation
		therefore conclude that it is safe to be near a rabbit.
31.	D. baby, child, teenager, adult, elder	This is the logical sequence of the human life cycle.
32.	A. 6	A dozen eggs is 12 eggs. 12/2=6.
33.	B. chart II	There are 2 triangles, 3 moons, 4 stars and 4 cylinders. This is shown on chart II.
34.	D. brother	The girl's uncle's father would be her grandfather. This means that the daughter of her grandfather could be her mother, and the 'daughter's son' could be the girl's brother. Since cousin was not given as an option, the only possible answer is brother.
35.	C. 125	Half of the diagram represents the owners of dogs which equals 500. Then the other half equals 500 and as we see that the purple is a $1/4$ of ½ the circle. 500/4 = 125 rabbits
36.	A. Jamaican geography	The passage discusses the location and the formation of Jamaica.
37.	B. top	If Jamaica is an island surrounded by water, it must be the top of the mountain that is positioned above the waterline.

ANSWERS AND EXPLANATIONS: 40–QUESTIONS TEST #2

Question	Answer	Explanation
38.	B. 3, 1	A polygon is a shape with at least three straight sides. Shape 1 is a circle with no straight sides, and shape 3 is not complete.
39.	A. 1/3	There are 6 equal parts and 2 parallelograms P (parallelogram) = 2/6 = 1/3
40.	B. 20	There are 2 triangles, so P (triangle) = 2/6 = 1/3 If we spin the wheel 60 times...times of P (triangle) = 1/3 * 60 = 20 times

How are you doing? Are you learning new information? Are you doing peer review sections?

Do what I do sometimes. I take a break and listen to one of my favourite songs, 'pick myself up, dust myself off and start all over again.'

See if you can find this reggae song - the remix of a son doing a tribute to his father.

ANSWERS AND EXPLANATIONS: 40-QUESTIONS TEST #3

40-QUESTIONS TEST #3

Answer key

Question	Answer	Explanation
1.	B. bird	They are all travelling stuff, but the bird is a creature.
2.	D. whale	They all lay eggs, except the whales who give birth to their babies.
3.	C. iodine	They all are metals, except iodine which is non-metal.
4.	A. Cuboid	They are all 2-dimensional shapes, except the cuboid which is a 3-dimensional shape.
5.	A. 1	A hexagon has 6 sides.
6.	C. 6	Sweets, chocolates and chips are fun to eat sometimes, but it is not good to eat them every day. These foods contain too much sugar, fat or salt. Fruits and vegetables help you to stay healthy and grow strong. • The first **and** should be replaced with a comma We use the comma to separate items in a series; **and** is used before the last item in a series. • **is** should be 'are'. 'Sweets, chocolates and chips' are the plural subject of the sentence and should be followed by a plural verb. • **but** should be ', but'. There should be a comma before **but**. • **these** should be 'These'. The sentence should begin with a capital letter.

ANSWERS AND EXPLANATIONS: 40–QUESTIONS TEST #3

Question	Answer	Explanation
		- helps should be 'help'. 'Fruit and vegetables' are the plural subject of the sentence and should be followed by a plural verb. - health should be 'healthy'. Health is a noun and cannot be used to describe the pronoun 'you'; hence, the adjective 'healthy' should be used.
7.	D. 18	The two bottom numbers are added to give the top one. Thus, 7 + 4 = 11 31=16 = 37 Then, 53 – 35 = 18
8.	D. horn	The only sound, among the four options, that is made by a car is the sound of a horn.
9.	B. leaf	A forest has many trees and a tree has many leaves.
10.	B. 1 hour 12 minutes	To find the time of the whole journey we add the bus's travelling time to the taxi's travelling time 23 + 49 = 72 minutes 1 hour = 60 minutes 72 – 60 = 12 minutes 72 minutes = 1 hour and 12 minutes.

ANSWERS AND EXPLANATIONS: 40-QUESTIONS TEST #3

Question	Answer	Explanation
11.	D. 12	Brad + Michael = 18 Brad has more 6 than Michael Brad + 6 = Michael = 18 Brad + 6 = 18 Brad = 18 − 6 = 12
12.	B. disagree	There could not be a right angle which equals $90°$ and an obtuse angle which is more than $90°$ in the same triangle. When the triangle has one obtuse angle. the other two angles should be acute angles which are less than $90°$.
13.	B. 40°	The sum of measurements of the interior angles of any triangle = $180°$. The right angle = $90°$. Then the third angle in the triangle = $180° − (90° + 50°) = 40°$.
14.	A. true	The giant tortoises and colourful crabs will be on channel 3, not 4.
15.	C. sports and documentary	Channel 4 is a sports channel. Channel 3 is a documentary channel.
16.	D. 16	The sum means to add while 'difference' means to take away (minus or subtract). 8 + 9 = 17; 9 − 8 = 1; 17 − 1 = 16
17.	C. easy	'Hard' and 'difficult' are synonyms, and 'simple' and 'easy' are synonyms.

ANSWERS AND EXPLANATIONS: 40-QUESTIONS TEST #3

Question	Answer	Explanation
18.	D. ratbats	Scientists say that Coronavirus originated in rat bats.
19.	B. calf	The baby cow is called a calf.
20.	A. luggage	Luggage is another name for travelling bags.
21.	C. DW	Combine the first and last letters of the alphabet successively.
22.	A. James	Brian and James have the greatest mark in Math. Michael has the greatest mark in science. James has the greatest mark in science and Math combined.
23.	C. Dwayne	Based on the graph and the key, Dwayne's math bar was the shortest, indicating that he had the lowest math score.
24.	B. telescope	A telescope is used to see very far things like the stars, but a microscope is used to see very small things to make it bigger.
25.	C. moment	Options A, B, and D aren't suitable. The right answer is a 'moment'.
26.	C. foal	The baby horse is called a foal.
27.	A. chart II	From the information, the number of fans is fewer than the number of TVs. This is represented only in chart II.
28.	B. false	The shows are about old and modern stories.
29.	C. shadow puppet theatres	The pronoun 'they' in the first line refers to 'shadow puppet theatres'.

ANSWERS AND EXPLANATIONS: 40-QUESTIONS TEST #3

Question	Answer	Explanation
30.	C. 10 litres	The answer will be the total cost divided by the cost per litre. $1,390 / 139 = 10 litres
31.	C. both are equal	Both of them weigh one kilogram, so they are equal.
32.	B. 41	Product means to multiply, and sum means to add. Here, we are adding twice. 6 x 5 = 30; 6 + 5 = 11; 30 + 11 = 41
33.	C. broke down	A car is a machine, so it breaks down.
34.	A. broke into	The thieves entered the bank illegally, so they broke into it.
35.	D. $20	The frame will cover the outside edges of the picture which equals the perimeter of the rectangle. The perimeter = 2 (base length + side length) The perimeter =2 (140 + 60) = 400 cm 400 cm = 4 metres The cost of 1 metre = $5 The cost of 4 metre = 5 * 4 = $20
36.	D. 1/4	The sample space S is given by S = {(H,T),(H,H),(T,H),(T,T)} Let E be the event 'two heads are obtained'. E = {(H,H)} We use the formula of the classical

Question	Answer	Explanation
		probability. P(E) = n(E) / n(S) = 1 / 4
37.	A. 1/26	There are 52 cards in the pack. Only one (1) card is a queen of club and only one (1) card is a king of hearts. So, the probability of pulling either card is 1/52 + 1/52 = 2/52. 2/52 = 1/26.
38.	B. 4,1,3,2	The logical sequence of making chocolate is Firstly, the cocoa plant is grown. Secondly, the cocoa beans are harvested from the plant. Thirdly, the cocoa beans are ground into powder. Finally, the powder is turned into chocolate with other ingredients.
39.	D. China	The line representing China on the graph remained at a constant during the third and fourth weeks, thus indicating that there was no increase in cases during this period.

ANSWERS AND EXPLANATIONS: 40-QUESTIONS TEST #3

Question	Answer	Explanation
40.	A. USA	In the fourth week, the line representing USA on the graph was at the highest point compared with those representing the other countries. This indicates that it had the greatest number of cases during the fourth week.

In case you were wondering, there is no app available that will take your exams for you. LOL ! But you can persevere! Believe you can and work hard. Come wid mi. Mek wi continue.

40-QUESTIONS TEST #4
Answer key

Question	Answer	Explanation
1.	C. tends	To tend is to care, look after, or pay attention to, as shepherds must do to keep their flock of sheep safe.
2.	A. flew	Flew is the past tense of fly, referring to how creatures with wings move through the air.
3.	D. squabbles	Squabbles can be a noun that refers to disagreements, but can also be a verb that describes the action of arguing.
4.	B. 40,571	40,571 would round up to 41,000 people, not 40,000.
5.	B. 20 to 39-year-olds	20 to 39-year-olds spend 300 hours per year socialising with 3 or fewer people, and 350 hours per year socialising with 4 or more people, making 650 hours per year in total.
6.	C. 100 hours	Adults over the age of 60 are spending 200 hours per year exercising alone, compared to the 100 hours per year teens spend exercising alone. 200-100=100 hours.
7.	C. Jada, Kevin, Ajani, Adam	It is stated that Adam is the tallest. Ajani is twice the height of Jada, making him second tallest as Kevin is 5 cm shorter than he is.

ANSWERS AND EXPLANATIONS: 40-QUESTIONS TEST #4

Question	Answer	Explanation
8.	B. butterfly	An egg develops into a caterpillar. A caterpillar develops into a chrysalis, from which a butterfly then emerges.
9.	C. holes	A sieve may have a handle, and may be made from metal or plastic, but without holes it would be unable to perform its function of separating solids.
10.	A. wings	An aeroplane may or may not have seats, a pilot, or windows, but must have wings to be considered an aeroplane.
11.	C. New Zealand	Auckland is described as the largest city on the north island of New Zealand.
12.	B. 1966	In 1966, the Commonwealth Games was hosted in Kingston.
13.	A. 1/4	$20/$80 = 1/4
14.	C. 62	Product 6 x 8 = 48 Sum 6 + 8 = 14 Answer = 48 +14 = 62.
15.	D. consecutive	If events take place 'in a row', they happen one after the other, or consecutively.
16.	B. a tennis player	An athlete is a person who competes in sports.
17.	A. Usain Bolt was drawn towards cricket	The writer uses the word 'interestingly' and the phrase 'in fact' to describe how Bolt was drawn to other sports before

ANSWERS AND EXPLANATIONS: 40–QUESTIONS TEST #4

Question	Answer	Explanation
	and football before athletics.	athletics, suggesting this is contradictory to what would have been expected.
18.	A. mother	Father, uncle and brother are all male relatives, whilst mother is a female relative.
19.	C. socks	Sandals, slippers and sneakers are all forms of shoes, whilst socks might be worn on the feet but are not shoes.
20.	D. discard	Terminate, end and finish all describe something coming to its final point, whilst discard means to get rid of something.
21.	B. Kingston, Jamaica, world, universe	Kingston a city in Jamaica. Jamaica is a country in the world, which is in the universe.
22.	D. 17 and 23	This is a list of the first 8 prime numbers from 2–23. A prime number can only be divided by itself and 1, without a reminder.
23.	C. 2018 saw the greatest numbers of visitors to Jamaica.	In 2018, cruise and armed forces visits dropped, but the number of stop-overs increased, making the total number of visitors the highest of all the years between 2005 and 2019.
24.	C. 7	Sum is 15 + 20 = 35; difference is 20 – 15 = 5. 35÷5 = 7
25.	B. R =7, P =5 and T= 6	The sum of all rows and column add up to 15.

ANSWERS AND EXPLANATIONS: 40-QUESTIONS TEST #4

Question	Answer	Explanation
		Hence using the columns 4 + R + 4 = !5. R = 15 - 8 = 7. Doing the same for P we get 5 + 5 + P = 15, where P works out to 5. Doing the same for T, we get T + 3 + 6 = 15, where T works out to 6.
26.	C. 4	The 4 tins of tomatoes will be present for every trip, meaning that 6 tins of pineapple can be transported each time. 6 tins x 4 trips = space to transport 24 tins in total, covering the 20 tins of pineapple required.
27.	D. 25	Each weight added to the spring is 2 kilograms. It will need 25 of these 2 kilogram weights to make 50 kilograms. 50 ÷ 2 = 25
28.	A. the weight required to sink the plastic toy boat	If Sam knows the weight required to sink the plastic toy boat, she can divide this weight by the weight of a single marble to accurately calculate how many marbles she will need altogether.
29.	B. 48	The number of sweets in the bag has to be divisible by 2 to get the number of red sweets, 4 to get the number of yellow sweets and 8 to get the number of green and purple sweets.
30.	D. CG + DF	The greatest length of all offered in the answers is CG, which runs along one edge of the square and one edge of the rectangle. The next greatest length is DF

ANSWERS AND EXPLANATIONS: 40–QUESTIONS TEST #4

Question	Answer	Explanation
		which is the diagonal of the rectangle. The two lengths added give the greatest length.
31.	C. 	Three quarters of the rectangle is shaded, which is the same as the circular segment which is three quarters of a whole circle.
32.	A. summer	While snow is a product of the cold winter season, sunshine is a product of the warm summer season.
33.	B. frog	While caterpillars are the younger form of butterflies, tadpoles are the younger form of frogs.
34.	D. late	While the opposite of wide is narrow, the opposite of early is late.
35.	A. smooth	While the opposite of stop is go, the opposite of rough is smooth.
36.	B. N and O	Pairing the letters of the alphabet with numbers (i.e. A=1, B=2, C=3 etc), odd letters will always appear on the right-hand pages, and even letters on the left. N is the fourteenth letter of the alphabet, appearing on the left-hand page, while O (the fifteenth letter) will face N on the right.
37.	C. 3, 5, 1, 4, 2	The raw ingredients shown in image 3, then the tomatoes are chopped up in image 5. The meat is grilled in image 1.

ANSWERS AND EXPLANATIONS: 40-QUESTIONS TEST #4

Question	Answer	Explanation
		Images 5 and 1 are interchangeable, but this is the only answer option with one then the other. Image 4 shows all the ingredients prepared and ready to assemble a burger. Whilst image 2 is of the final burger being assembled, ready to serve.
38.	B. chart II.	Reading and gaming have equal sized segments, which are both smaller than the segment representing playing football. By far, the biggest segment of the circle is playing with friends.
39.	A. The orange box can hold the same number of 1 cm cubes as the blue box.	Capacity of box = length x width x height The capacity of the orange box is 24 cm^3 (6cm x 2cm x 2cm). The capacity of the blue box is also 24 cm^3 (4cm x 3cm x 2cm). They can both, therefore, hold the same number of cubes.
40.	C. J$600	The sweets segment is one eighth of the chart. Book/magazines are represented by half of the chart, or four-eighths, so 4 x J$150 is J$600 spent on books and magazines.

40–QUESTIONS TEST #5

Answer key

Question	Answer	Explanation
1.	B. 11	The sequence follows the pattern of subtracting 3 from one number in the chain, making the answer the next number in the chain, then adding 5 to the answer to make the next number in the chain. E.g. **10** -3 = **7** +5 = 12 **12** -3 = **9** + 5 = 14 **14** -3 = **11**
2.	B. 15,602	15,602 would round up to 16,000 people, not 15,000.
3.	D. FH + EH	The longest length of all is the diagonal FH, followed by the line EH. Adding these two lengths together will therefore give the greatest length of all.
4.	A. 140 units	Every mark on the cylinder is 10 units. There are 4 marks above 100 units, so the arrow is pointed at 140 units.
5.	B. 75	The rule of the sequence is x2 (multiply by 2). This is a doubling of the previous number added. For example, in the sequence, the rule is 5, 5+**10**=15, 15+**20**=35, 35+**40**=75, 75+**80**=155, 155+**160**=355

Question	Answer	Explanation
6.	D. 	Switch the position of the diagonals.
7.	D. Thomas' father is Brian's brother.	Visualising the family tree, gives the following diagram: ? — Brian Amanda — ? Alan Thomas Thomas' father is unknown. Brian has only ONE sibling, his sister, Amanda.
8.	C. tremendous	Tremendous describes something very big or a large amount. Since there has been so much rain that flooding has occurred, tremendous is the best word to complete the sentence.
9.	B. elect	To elect a leader into power involves the people voting on who they would like to take the position.
10.	D. choir	A choir is a group of singers, who very often rehearse together to organise their voices in a melodic way.
11.	B. Errol, Gloria, Sonia, Donald	It is stated that Errol rolled the highest even number, which must be 8. Gloria scored one less than Errol, so that must be 7. Donald rolled an odd number less than 4, so that's either 3 or 1. If Donald

ANSWERS AND EXPLANATIONS: 40–QUESTIONS TEST #5

Question	Answer	EXPLANATION
		rolled a 3, Sonia scored 6 (double Donald's score) putting her 3rd highest, or if he rolled a 1, she scored 2, again making her 3rd highest. Donald's is therefore the lowest score.
12.	C. 7	The crew of 2 people will be present for every crossing, meaning that 6 passengers can be transported each time. 6 passengers x 7 pickups = 42 passengers potentially transported in total, covering the 40 required.
13.	A. true	If Indonesia has plantations producing palm oil, these plantations must be growing palm oil trees.
14.	D. unable to tell	While we are told the percentage of forested land in Indonesia, we are not told the number of hectares this covers. Depending on the size of Indonesia, this could be more or fewer trees than Jamaica.
15.	C. musicians	An orchestra may include a violin, may perform on a stage and may follow sheet music, but must include more than one musician to be considered an orchestra.
16.	D. wind	A storm system is called a hurricane because of its wind speed.
17.	B. 16	Since there are only black and white cars in the car park and for every white car there are 2 black cars,

ANSWERS AND EXPLANATIONS: 40-QUESTIONS TEST #5

Question	Answer	Explanation
		then 2/3 of the cars are black. Hence the answer is 24 x 2/3 =16 black cars.
18.	B. 4	The number in the middle of the triangle is the sum of the numbers at each corner. Hence, to find the missing number 15 − (3 + 8) = 4, The missing number is 4.
19.	B △	Follow the pattern taking note of the up and down triangles. The next in the sequence is an upward pointed triangle.
20.	C. always	'Never' describes something that has not happened at any time. 'Sometimes' refers to something that happens, but not very often, while 'often' implies something occurs many times. 'Always' is the word needed to describe an event taking place more than often, in fact all the time!
21.	C. spoon	'Paper, pencil and ink' are all types of stationery, while a spoon is an eating utensil.
22.	B. walk	'Fly, hover and glide' all describe movement through the air, whilst 'walk' describes movement on the ground.
23.	C. cuddle	'Bully, torment and harass' are ways of making another person suffer, whilst to cuddle a person is to show affection.

ANSWERS AND EXPLANATIONS: 40-QUESTIONS TEST #5

Question	Answer	Explanation
24.	C. square-based pyramid	The square-base of the pyramid is shown in the middle of the net.
25.	B. 96	From the diagram, the 32 dogs represent 1/3 the total number of students with pets. Hence the total number of students with pets is 32 x 3 =96.
26.	C. the number of mangoes that will be placed into one crate	If Kate knows the number of mangoes that will be placed into one crate, she can divide 500 by this number to estimate how many crates she will need altogether.
27.	A. chart I	There are 19 triangles altogether. Only one of the triangles is green, and there are equal amounts (6) of each of the other three colours.
28.	D. Book borrowing has decreased in Town A.	In January, more than 400 books were borrowed in Town A. Over the year, this gradually decreased until there were little more than 50 books borrowed in December.
29.	B. hurlftgifik	If 'hurlftteut' means cook dinner, and 'jopuphurlft' means vegetarian cook, we may expect 'hurlft' to mean 'cook', and therefore be at the start of the word that means 'cook fish'. While we have no way of knowing what 'gifik' means, there is only one option with 'hurlft', so we can infer that 'gifik' means 'fish'.
30.	B. feeding	To graze means to feed, usually on grass.

ANSWERS AND EXPLANATIONS: 40–QUESTIONS TEST #5

Question	Answer	Explanation
31.	D. The manatee has many natural predators.	The passage states that the manatee has no natural predator.
32.	D. The manatee is an amazing creature.	All the other answers are facts. Answer D is an opinion.
33.	A. 16 and 17	Even-numbered pages will always be on the left-hand side, and odd-numbered pages on the right.
34.	A. 3 and 5	5 + 3 = 8 5 - 3 = 2
35.	D. sunrise, day, sunset, night	When the sun rises, day begins. At the end of the day, the sun sets, bringing night.
36.	C. chart III	The biggest segment represents children with no siblings, and a segment half the size represents children with one sibling. The two segments left are the smallest but are also equally sized, to represent the same number of children having 2 or 3 brothers or sisters.
37.	C. wolf	While a group of birds is a flock, a group of wolves is a pack.
38.	A. stove	While a car is located in a garage, a stove is located in a kitchen.
39.	C. conceal	While sad means the same thing as unhappy, conceal means the same thing as hide.

ANSWERS AND EXPLANATIONS: 40-QUESTIONS TEST #5

Question	Answer	Explanation
40.	B. cold	While big and enormous are both degrees of size, cold and freezing are both degrees of temperature.

Did you know that 'a river cuts through a rock not because of its power, but because of its persistence'?

- James N. Watkins

How is this applicable to you?

40-QUESTIONS TEST #6

Answer key

Question	Answer	Explanation
1.	A. strings	A guitar may be played by a musician, may produce sound, and may be played with a plectrum, but without strings, the instrument could not be classified as a guitar.
2.	D. food	A meal may include bread and a drink, and may be eaten using cutlery, but it must include a substantial amount of food to be classified as a meal.
3.	A. room, house, street, town	A room is found in a house, and a house upon a street. A number of streets together make up a town.
4.	C. 5	A crew of 5 people will be present on every flight, meaning that 23 passengers can be transported on each flight with them. 23 tourists x 5 flights = 115 passengers potentially transported in total, covering the 100 required.
5.	A. Devan, Justin, Tianna, Amoy	It is stated that Devan is 10 years old. Tianna is 2 years older than Devan, so she must be 12 years old. Amoy is 3 years older than Devan, making Amoy 13 years old and the eldest. Finally, Justin is two years older than Tianna was three years ago. If Tianna is 12 years old, she was 9 three years ago, so Justin is two years older than that (11 years old). Justin is therefore, one year older than Devan, making Devan the youngest.

Question	Answer	Explanation
6.	B. Jamaica	In the Northwest Pacific Basin, strong tropical storms are known as typhoons. Jamaica is found in the Atlantic Basin where the term typhoon is not used.
7.	B. The storms are seasonal in Jamaica, while they are all year round in the Northwest Pacific Basin.	The best option is B. Extract 1 describes the storm season in the Northwest Pacific Basin, describing its length, countries it affects and the number of systems the region has annually. Extract 2 describes the storm season in Jamaica describing its length and how likely Jamaica is to be hit.
8.	A. All three nets could be folded to make a cube.	Each of the 3 nets has 6 faces which can be folded to make a cube. In total, a cube has 11 possible nets!
9.	C. the seventh row	Each row holds 12 seats. Row 1 will be seats 1 to 12, row 2 seats 13 to 24 and so on. Therefore, to speed things up, we can multiply each row number by 12. Row 5 x 12 = 60, so Lucinda's seat must be further back. Row 6 x 12 = 72, so seats 61 to 72 must be in this row...again, not Lucind's seat. Row 7 x 12 = 84, so row 7 has seats 73 to 84, which includes Lucind's seat (number 79).
10.	A. ➡ ★ ○	In the analogy you have been presented with, the centre shape remains untouched. The bottom shape switches places with the top shape and is black rather than white, while the shape which has moved to the bottom is white rather than black.

ANSWERS AND EXPLANATIONS: 40–QUESTIONS TEST #7

Question	Answer	Explanation
11.	D. 11	The art segment is one eighth of the chart. Fiction books are represented by $1/2$ of the chart, or $4/8$. So if 44 fiction books were borrowed, 44 divided by 4 is equal to 11 art books borrowed.
12.	B. the time it takes to make one laptop	If the factory manager knows the time it takes to make 1 laptop, he can divide the 8 hours by the time needed to make 1 laptop, and accurately calculate how many laptops the machine can make per shift.
13.	A. whale	A mosquito is a very small creature, while a rabbit is much bigger than a mosquito, and an elephant is much bigger than a rabbit. A whale is a creature much bigger than an elephant.
14.	C. Mangoes cost more than bananas and coconuts.	We are told that bananas cost less than mangoes. If bananas cost more than coconuts, coconuts must also cost less than mangoes.
15.	C. week 3	Adding the sales of grater cake and peanut cake together, week 3 sales were 88 cakes, compared to 70 cakes in week 4, 67 cakes in week 2 and 64 cakes in week 1.
16.	B. coconut drops	Coconut drops sales were 32 in week 1, and 55 in week 4, which is an increase of 23 sales, compared to an increase of 22 grater cake sales which saw the second highest rise.
17.	A. 99,367	99,367 would round down to 99,000 people, not up to 100,000.

ANSWERS AND EXPLANATIONS: 40–QUESTIONS TEST #7

Question	Answer	Explanation
18.	D. Coconut sales remained steady throughout the month.	In week 1, around 100 coconuts were sold. Just under 100 coconuts were sold in week 2 and just over 100 in week 3. In week 4, sales of coconuts were back around the 100 mark, showing that the sales were steady throughout the month.
19.	C. ghedkscvvpo	If 'ghedkriidr' means face forward, and 'asdonghedk' means smiley face, we may expect 'ghedk' to mean 'face', and therefore be at the start of the word that means 'facemask'. While we have no way of knowing what 'scvvpo' means, there is only one option with 'ghedk' at the start, so we can assume that 'scvvpo' means 'mask'.
20.	B. desert	While grass is the thing and green is its characteristic, desert is the thing that pairs with the characteristic dry.
21.	A. buy	While 'eat' is the present tense verb and 'ate' its past tense form, 'buy' is the present tense verb that pairs with the past tense form 'bought'.
22.	D. fire	While 'plant' is the cause and 'grow' its effect, 'fire' is the cause that has 'burn' as an effect.
23.	A. laugh	While graceful is the opposite of clumsy, laugh is the opposite of cry.
24.	C. 70, 38	The rule of the sequence is -16. For example, the first number in the sequence is 102, and the second 86. 102-16=86. Following this rule, 86-70=16, and 54-16=38.

ANSWERS AND EXPLANATIONS: 40–QUESTIONS TEST #7

Question	Answer	Explanation
25.	D. yearly	Annual means occurring once each year.
26.	B. diamonds	A 'sought-after' item is in high demand due to its rarity or exceptional quality.
27.	A. Blue Mountain coffee is smooth and delicate.	The writer uses the words 'smooth' and 'delicate' to describe the coffee's flavour and agrees that its reputation for being one of the best coffees in the world is 'well-deserved.'
28.	A. 5	If we multiply ½ X 6 = 3 and 3 x 6 = 18. Hence we divide 30 by 6 to get the answer =5.
29.	A. tens	200-21 =179. Hence the digit 7 is at the tens place.
30.	B. 2.75	The dot occurs after point 2.50. The only option for greater than 2.50 is 2.75.
31.	D. roar	'Squeak, cheep, and tweet' are all high-pitched, short sounds made by animals, whilst roar is a long, deep animal sound.
32.	B. sunshine	'Rain, hail and snow' are all forms of precipitation, whilst sunshine is a form of light.
33.	C. crouch	'Leap, bound and spring' all describe jumping, whilst to crouch is to bend your knees and upper body down, firmly on the floor.
34.	B. SX + RX	SX and RX are the two shortest lengths on the diagram, so adding them together would give the shortest overall length of all of the sums offered as answers.

ANSWERS AND EXPLANATIONS: 40–QUESTIONS TEST #7

Question	Answer	Explanation
35.	C. cousins	John and Tom are cousins. Since Mary is John's sister, then she is also Tom's cousin.
36.	C. 2, 1, 3, 4, 5	Eggs are shown in image 2, with a chick starting to break through the shell in image 1. The chick is out of the egg in image 3, and larger and feeding in image 4. In image 5, the chick is fully grown and flying.
37.	D. 14	The sum of the pair of numbers in the yellow boxes is the same as the sum of the pair of numbers in the green boxes. In the last diagram, the sum of the numbers in the green boxes is 20 (11+9). The sum of the numbers in the yellow boxes therefore also needs to be 20. If one of the numbers is 6, the other number must be 14, as 6+14=20. OR Add/Subtract the same number from each diagonal in the pair. For the first set, add 5 i.e. (5 + 4 = 9 and 5 + 3 = 8). For the second set, add 3 to 5 and 7. For the third set, subtract 5 from 11 to get 6. Subtract 5 from the unknown to get 9. Hence, the unknown is 5 + 9 =14.
38.	C. remedy	A remedy is a medicine used to cure or relieve an ailment or disease. It can also be the solution to a problem.
39.	B. scene	A section of action in a film or play is known as a scene.
40.	D. 16	Sequence follows the pattern: add 3, then subtract 2, then repeat.

40-QUESTIONS TEST #7
Answer key

Question	Answer	Explanation
1.	C. 10:30 am	If the journey takes exactly the 2 hours 45 minutes expected, Nicola will arrive in Montego Bay at 11:00 am. It is reasonable to estimate that the bus may be 5 minutes early or 15 minutes late, but 30 minutes early is the unlikeliest time Nicola could expect to arrive.
2.	D. 45	If each team must have exactly 5 players and 1 coach, the number of people competing must be a multiple of 6, which 45 is not.
3.	B. words	Language may be presented as speech or text, and can involve using your tongue if it is spoken, but without words there is no language.
4.	A. treatment	A 'nurse, medication and stethoscope' may all be very useful to have in a hospital, but without treatment there is no hospital.
5.	B. thousands	963 + 487 = 1450. The digit 1 is in the thousands place.
6.	B. prepare, cook, serve, eat	Food is first prepared (e.g. washed, chopped, seasoned and so on), and then

ANSWERS AND EXPLANATIONS: 40–QUESTIONS TEST #7

Question	Answer	Explanation
		cooked. Once cooked, the food can be served and eaten.
7.	A. $185	Cost of books = $80 x 2 = $160 Pens = $40 x 2 = $80 pencils = $20 x 3 = $60 sharpener = $15 x 1 = $15 Total = $315 Change = $500 - $315 = $185
8.	D. book	While fingers are part of the hand, pages are part of a book.
9.	A. table	While lunch can be classified as a meal, a table can be classified as furniture.
10.	B. knife	While the function of a pen is to write, the function of a knife is to cut.
11.	C. itch	While the problem of being hungry can be solved by having something to eat, the problem of an itch can be solved by giving it a scratch.
12.	C. JM + KM	The greatest length of all is KM, which runs vertically down the centre of the kite. JM appears to be the second longest length (along with LM), and so adding KM to either of the two would result in the greatest length of all.
13.	C. 6	The crew of 3 people will be present for every crossing, meaning that 9

ANSWERS AND EXPLANATIONS: 40–QUESTIONS TEST #7

Question	Answer	Explanation
		passengers can be transported each time (12 - 3 = 9). 9 passengers x 6 trips = 54 passengers potentially transported in total, covering the 53 required.
14.	D. Amelia must head south on Market St. and west on Bridge St. to reach school.	
15.	D. U and V	Considering the placement of the letters within the alphabet, odd letters will always appear on the left-hand pages, and even letters on the right. For example, A is the 1st letter (an odd number) and so appears on the left. C is the 3rd letter, again odd and appearing on the left. Since U is the 21st letter of the alphabet, which is an odd number, it appears on the left-hand page. V (the 22nd letter) has an even alphabet placing, and will face U on the right.
16.	A. chart I	The biggest segment represents most of the students liking sci-fi movies, while the tiny segment represents those who prefer dramas. The segment for comedies is bigger than the segment for

ANSWERS AND EXPLANATIONS: 40-QUESTIONS TEST #7

Question	Answer	Explanation
		romances, and the remaining segment (not the biggest or the smallest) shows the rest of the students who enjoy action movies.
17.	B. paragraph	A group of organised letters form a word, and a group of organised words form a sentence. A paragraph is formed by an organised group of sentences.
18.	A. carnival, which involves parties and parades	Carnival arose in Trinidad and Tobago in the 1700s and in Jamaica in the 1940s. That is about a 200 year difference, so option A is true. Options B and C did not address the history of Carnival in both extracts, and option D is false.
19.	B. 1990	Carnival did not begin in Jamaica until 1990.
20.	C. 2, 4, 5, 3, 1	Farmers are ploughing the field ready for planting in image 2, while the seeds are sown in image 4. Image 5 shows the growing crops, which are harvested in image 3. Finally, the corn is served with chicken in image 1.
21.	D. The weight of one brick.	If Billy knows the weight of one brick, he can divide one tonne by the weight of a single brick to calculate how many bricks he can expect to arrive.
22.	C. 100	Product $6 \times 8 = 48$

ANSWERS AND EXPLANATIONS: 40-QUESTIONS TEST #7

Question	Answer	Explanation
		Double 48 x 2 = 96 Sum 6 + 8 = 12 Adding sum 96 + 12 = 108 108 to the nearest hundred = 100
23.	B. prevent	Prevent means to stop. As the police are trying to stop crime, prevent is the best word to complete the sentence.
24.	C. paws	An animal's foot with claws and pads is known as a paw. Paws is the plural form of this word.
25.	B. capsized	If a boat has capsized, it has turned over in the water.
26.	C. 9	A third of the pens are black, which would be 3 pens out of 9. There are half the number of red pens compared to blue, so 1 red pen and 2 blue pens. That is 3 + 1 + 2 = 6 pens so far. The rest are green and there are 3 pens left over, but there has to be an even number of green pens, and 3 is an odd number.
27.	A. lisdssjifd	This is the only option beginning with the word 'lisds' meaning pitch since: 'jlxat' means water proof 'lisds' means pitch 'spacb' means tent 'wueeh' means football

ANSWERS AND EXPLANATIONS: 40-QUESTIONS TEST #7

Question	Answer	Explanation
28.	B. Club B saw a sharp decrease in the number of attendees between May and August.	In May, the number of attendees at club B was 400 people, which dropped to 100 people by August.
29.	C. 30	The bus segment is one eighth of the chart. The children who travel by bike are represented by a segment double this size (2 eighths, or a quarter), so if 15 children take the bus, double the number of children ride bikes to school. 15 x 2 = 30.
30.	C. Carmen, Monica, Roy, Edward	It is stated that Monica takes 5 minutes to ride to the shops. If Roy takes twice as long as Monica, he takes ten minutes. Edward takes 2 minutes longer than Roy, which is 12 minutes and the slowest time overall. Carmen takes 6 minutes less than Roy, which is 10 – 6 = 4 minutes, making her the winner of the bike ride race.
31.	B. ★ (star with circle)	In the analogy you have been presented with, the outer shape stays the same. The inner triangle grows in size and changes position with the circle, which shrinks and is now white rather than black. The answer, therefore, also requires the star to grow in size and change position with

ANSWERS AND EXPLANATIONS: 40-QUESTIONS TEST #7

Question	Answer	Explanation
		the cross, while the cross shrinks and is now white rather than black. same outer shape enlarged star
32.	C. suitably	If something is described as 'fitting,' it means it is suitable, or proper under the circumstances.
33.	A. beach	A distraction is something that makes it difficult for a person to concentrate. The passage stated that the writer faced the wall, so he won't be distracted. Generally, a beach would not be a distraction but based on the passage and the other choices, A is correct.
34.	D. Fleming's villa is a beautiful place.	The writer uses the words 'gorgeous' and 'luxury' to describe Fleming's villa, suggesting that it is a beautiful place.
35.	C. 2½	If ½ is represented by the number 10, and 50 is 5 x 10, this means 50 is also 5 x ½ = 2½.
36.	D. paw	'Fur, fleece and hair' are all animal coverings, whilst a paw is an animal's foot.
37.	B. skull	'Heart, kidney and liver' are all organs, whilst the skull is a bone.

ANSWERS AND EXPLANATIONS: 40-QUESTIONS TEST #7

Question	Answer	Explanation
38.	A. touch	'Smooth, rough and soft' all describe texture, whilst touch is to use a part of your body to feel something.
39.	A. 51 mm	The second largest bird is the duck (3500 g), with an egg length of 76 mm, while the second smallest bird is the mockingbird (60 g), with an egg length of 25 mm. 76 – 25 = 51 mm.
40.	D. 3	One week is 7 days, so 3 weeks is 21 days. The eggs of the mockingbird, the hummingbird and the chicken hatch in less than 21 days.

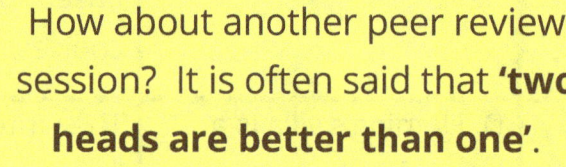

How about another peer review session? It is often said that **'two heads are better than one'**.

Do you remember what to do? If not, review page 110 again. You can both decide the number of questions you want to review together.

Have fun while you learn from each other.

ANSWERS AND EXPLANATIONS: 40-QUESTIONS TEST #8

40-QUESTIONS TEST #8
Answer key

Question	Answer	Explanation
1.	B. Jamil, Joyce, Lloyd, Gilda	Gilda takes the longest, so Lloyd's journey of 25 minutes must be shorter than hers. Jamil's journey takes half the time of Lloyd's, so that's 12.5 minutes. The shortest journey of all, Joyce's, is just 5 minutes quicker than Lloyd's, so her journey must take 20 minutes, a shorter journey than Lloyd's and Gilda's, but $7\frac{1}{2}$ minutes longer than Jamil.
2.	B. 4, 3, 1, 2, 5	The plans for building a home feature in image 4, while the foundations are laid in image 3. Image 1 shows the house almost built, and in image 2 it is complete. In image 5, a family is moving into their new home.
3.	A. 8	The water play segment is one eighth of the chart. Outdoor play is represented by $\frac{1}{2}$ of the chart, or $\frac{4}{8}$, and represents 32 children. Therefore, 32 divided by 4 is 8 children who prefer to play with water.
4.	A. bear	To bear means to withstand.
5.	C. 2019	In 2019, 80 men swam at the beach per day, along with 50 children. Assuming 50% of the 50 children were male, 80 men + 25

ANSWERS AND EXPLANATIONS: 40-QUESTIONS TEST #8

Question	Answer	Explanation
		boys = 105 male swimmers and the most over the 4-year period.
6.	B. 35	In total, 245 men swam at the beach (60 + 50 + 80 + 55), compared to 210 women (35 + 50 + 60 + 65). So, 35 more men swam at the beach when compared to women (245 to 210).
7.	A. the number of bacteria in the petri dish at the start	If Alexa knows the number of bacteria in the petri dish at the start, she can double this number to find out how many will be in the dish after 20 minutes, then double this answer to find the number of bacteria in the dish after 40 minutes, and so on until she has accurately calculated how many bacteria will be in the dish after 2 hours.
8.	D. chart IV	Combining the segments for strawberry and raspberry shows fruit as the most liked flavour of all. The sections representing strawberry and vanilla flavours are both the same size, and chocolate (the least liked flavour) is the smallest segment of all.
9.	B. 1	If 2 gives 16, then 1 gives 8, therefore, the answer is 1.
10.	C. *ohmagimsytb*	'Ohmagimsytb' means sunflower plant because: 'haif' means seed 'msytbgi' means plant 'ohmagi' means sunflower

ANSWERS AND EXPLANATIONS: 40-QUESTIONS TEST #8

Question	Answer	Explanation
		'baslp' means potted.
11.	C. brush	While you hammer a nail, you brush your hair.
12.	C. scaly	While courage is a defining characteristic of a hero, scaly skin is a defining characteristic of an iguana.
13.	D. orange	While happiness is classified as an emotion, an orange is classified as a fruit.
14.	A. laughing	While trembling is a sign of fear, laughing is a sign of amusement.
15.	D. 14	If a $\frac{1}{4}$ of the flowers are red, the total number of flowers in the bunch needs to be a multiple of 4. 14 is not a multiple of 4, so a $\frac{1}{4}$ of 14 flowers would be $3\frac{1}{2}$ and cannot represent whole flowers.
16.	B. 2	In each circle, the sum of the top numbers and the bottom left numbers is equal to the number on the bottom right. i.e. $1 + 4 + 5 = 10$ $2 + 3 + 7 = 12$ So $? + 8 + 3 = 13$ $? + 11 = 13$ $? = 13 - 11$ $? = 2$

ANSWERS AND EXPLANATIONS: 40–QUESTIONS TEST #8

Question	Answer	Explanation
17.	D. Edward	Putting the information into diagrammatic form, the family's relationships are as follows: Adam and Clara ——————— Edward (husband and wife) (Clara's brother) Dana Bradley Freddie (Adam and Clara's children) If Edward is Dana's mother's brother, then he is Dana's uncle.
18.	A. advanced	'Cutting-edge' describes the most advanced stage of development, with all the newest technology.
19.	B. a space flight operations facility	A 'specialist' focuses on a specific, often highly skilled, subject or activity. A space flight operations facility is therefore a specialist facility, because it is a place that focuses on activities not carried out anywhere else.
20.	D. The hospital's department for treating heart disease is very impressive.	The writer uses the word 'remarkable' to describe the new cardiac facility, suggesting the writer thinks it is extraordinary and very impressive.
21.	D. ones	62 x 5 = 310. The digit 0 is in the ones place.
22.	D. NO + PQ	PQ is the shortest length of the diagram. There seems to be very little difference

ANSWERS AND EXPLANATIONS: 40–QUESTIONS TEST #8

Question	Answer	Explanation
		between the next shortest lengths (LO and LQ) so adding PQ to either of them would result in the shortest length overall.
23.	A. m	Sequence follows the pattern skip 1 letter, then skip 2 letters, then skip 1 letter. Continue this pattern.
24.	C. If Noel heads north on St Andrew's street and east on High Street, he will reach the park.	
25.	A. 1	We know that triangles have 3 sides and rectangles have 4 sides. If one of the shapes is a triangle (3 sides), there are 8 sides remaining (11 sides – 3 sides). Since 8 is a multiple of 4, it could represent 2 rectangles (8 ÷ 4 = 2). Checking the other answers, the number of sides would not leave a multiple of 4, and so cannot be the number of triangles Peter is sorting.
26.	A. lizard	Turtle, manatee and shark are all creatures which live in water, whilst a lizard lives on land.
27.	C. donate	Rob, thieve and steal all describe taking something from someone, whilst to donate

Question	Answer	Explanation
		is to give something, rather than take it away.
28.	C. hammer	Repair, mend and fix all describe restoring something to good condition, whilst to hammer is to hit something repeatedly.
29.	D. 792	A guess of 792 is only 3 sweets away from the actual amount of 789, and is therefore the closest guess.
30.	B. plough	To plough is to turn over soil with machinery in preparation for sowing seeds.
31.	C. employ	To offer work to someone in exchange for payment is to employ them.
32.	C. swarming	'Swarming' describes moving in a large group, such as the 'swarming' of wasps. As the market is very busy, 'swarming' is the best word to complete the sentence.
33.	D. 7	A staff of 3 people will be present on every bus, meaning that 15 tourists can be transported on each bus with them. 15 tourists x 7 buses = 105 tourists potentially transported in total, covering the 100 required.
34.	D.	In the analogy you have been presented with, the trapezium at the bottom has switched places with the trapezium at the top. The arrows must therefore do the same, so the black arrow pointing upwards

ANSWERS AND EXPLANATIONS: 40–QUESTIONS TEST #8

Question	Answer	Explanation
		goes on top, and the white arrow pointing down moves to the bottom.
35.	C. Jamaica has a football team that plays international matches.	Jamaica contributes its best players to the West Indies Cricket Team, an international representation of many countries in the Caribbean region.
36.	B. 2015	The Concacaf Gold Cup is a football tournament where the final was reached by the Reggae Boyz in 2015 and 2017.
37.	D. leopard, cat, mammal, animal	A leopard is a type of cat. Cats are a group of mammals, and mammals are warm-blooded animals.
38.	C. 81	The rule of the sequence is $3^1 = 3$, $3^2 = 9$, $3^3 = 27$, $3^4 = 81$, $3^5 = 243$ and $3^6 = 729$.
39.	D. water	Swimming may involve wearing a swimming costume, using a towel, and could take place in the ocean, but without water, it is impossible to swim.
40.	C. trees	A forest may have grass, wildlife and leaves, but without any trees the area would not be called a forest.

40-QUESTIONS TEST #9

Answer key

Question	Answer	Explanation
1.	C. 17	Grid one has sequential even numbers: 10, 12, 14, 16. Grid two has sequential odd numbers: 11, 13, 15, 17. Grid three has sequential prime numbers: 11, 13, 17, 19.
2.	B. The price of the oranges was incorrect on the receipt.	This sentence has the only correct spelling of the word in question: R-E-C-E-I-P-T
3.	A. 19	We added 1, 1, 2, 2, 3, 3, 4, as follows: 3 + 1 = 4 + 1= 5 + 2 = 7 + 2 = 9 + 3 = 12 + 3 = 15 + 4 = 19
4.	A. 80	Combined age in 7 years is 92. In four years' time: 7 x 4 = 28. Therefore, the combined age now is 92 - 28 = 64. In four years, the age is 64 + 4 x 4 = 80.
5.	C. 2/5	The number line is divided into 5 parts. The dot is on the second partition = 2/5.
6.	B. False	If the first two are true, then Tommy is the youngest. Therefore, the third sentence must be false.
7.	C. III, II, IV, I	When preparing for a test, we first get to know what the test is about, gather the notes, study for the test then, sit the test.

ANSWERS AND EXPLANATIONS: 40–QUESTIONS TEST #9

Question	Answer	Explanation
8.	D. 42	Given that there are three different colours, an easy approach is to review the answer choices, A through D, and see which choice could be divided by 3 without leaving a remainder. Choice D, 42, divided by 3, gives you 14. So, there are 14 reds, 14 blue and 14 yellow towels.
9.	A. 2 hours and 24 minutes	Travel to school and home again is two trips: (23 x2) minutes on the bus plus (46 x 2) minutes in the taxi equals 144 minutes which is 2 hours and 24 minutes.
10.	A. niece and uncle	Abigay is Mary's daughter. Mary's sister, Lois, is Abigay's aunt. So, Lois's husband John, is Abigay's uncle.
11.	B. first cousins	Brian is Mary's son. Mary's sister is Lois. Daniel is Lois's son. So, Daniel and Brian are first cousins.
12.	C. 9 minutes	It takes 9 minutes because he needs to make 9 cuts to get 10 sections.
13.	B. went	Went is the past tense of go.
14.	D. 5	Subtract 1, 2, 3 then subtract 4. 15 – 1 = 14, 14 – 2 = 12
15.	C. 2	Subtract ½ from the number before.
16.	B. Tuesday	Counting back 4 days before Monday is Thursday. If Thursday is the day after tomorrow, tomorrow must be Wednesday and today is Tuesday.
17.	B. absent	Well is the opposite of sick and present is the opposite of absent.

www.mycheetahacademy.com

Question	Answer	Explanation
18.	C. 4 km	The journey is illustrated as a sketch. Their footsteps form the following incomplete rectangle:  If the man walks 4 km east, he would be back at his starting point.
19.	A. JQ	Use alternate letters from the start and the end of the alphabet. For example, we will not use A and Z, but the letters B and Y. We would skip C and X and use DW and so on.
20.	C. 9	A staff of 2 people will be present on every helicopter trip, meaning that 6 tourists can be catered for each sightseeing tour if the capacity of the helicopter is 8 people in total. 6 tourists x 9 tours = 54 tourists in total, covering the 50 required.
21.	C. wealth	An antonym is a word with the opposite meaning. Poverty is the state of being extremely poor, so an abundance of money or possessions is the opposite meaning.
22.	C. books	A library is a room or an entire building which contains books. It may or may not have windows, people visiting the space, and shelves to store the books upon.
23.	D. wall - fence	The whole is related to the parts, except for wall and fence

ANSWERS AND EXPLANATIONS: 40-QUESTIONS TEST #9

Question	Answer	Explanation
24.	D. push - shove	All are the opposite of each other except for push and shove which are similar in meaning
25.	D. light - fight	All the words sound alike but have different meanings and spellings except for light-fight, which are related because they rhyme.
26.	C. 30	20 x 12 = 240 20 – 12 = 8 Answer 40 ÷ 8 = 30
27.	C. 4:30	To each clock add +47 minutes, so the last one is 4:30.
28.	B. 2 books, 3 pens, 3 pencils and 1 sharpener	(2 x $50) + (3 x $30) + (3 x $25) + (1 x $25) = $290
29.	C. Daniel is Cecilia's brother.	Putting the information into diagrammatic form, the family's relationships are as follows: Bill (Cecilia's father) — Amanda (Cecilia's husband's mother) Daniel (Cecilia's brother) — Cecilia & Edward (Cecilia's husband) If Daniel is the son of Bill and Cecilia is Bill's daughter, then Daniel and Cecilia are brother and sister.

ANSWERS AND EXPLANATIONS: 40–QUESTIONS TEST #9

Question	Answer	Explanation
30.	D. heel, knee, chest, face	The heel, on the bottom of the foot, is the body part closest to the ground. The knee follows next, halfway up the leg. The chest is the next highest body part, and finally the face.
31.	A. filthy	Calm is a synonym of peaceful. So we use filthy as a synonym of dirty.
32.	C. tape	The last three letters of boat and goat are -oat. The only word with the same last three letters as escape is tape.
33.	D. unable to tell	While we are told that more than 600,000 fans visit Graceland each year, and that Nine Mile is a 'sleepy Jamaican town', we do not know for certain the number of fans visiting Nine Mile, and so we are unable to tell.
34.	D. lion	All the options are young animals except 'lion'.
35.	A. leaf	A branch, root and trunk are all necessary parts of a tree, which is the whole. Of the four options, only a leaf is also a necessary part of a tree. A petal is a necessary part of a flower rather than a tree, which may or may not produce flowers. Trees grow in dirt and may be surrounded by grass, but these are also not necessary parts of the tree.
36.	D. 78 cm	Sheree is three times smaller than Abe. If Abe is 180 cm tall, 180 divided by 3 is 60, making Sheree 60 cm tall. If Sheree is 18 cm shorter than Michael, Michael is 18 cm taller than her. 60 + 18 = 78, making Michael 78 cm tall.

ANSWERS AND EXPLANATIONS: 40–QUESTIONS TEST #9

Question	Answer	Explanation
37.	C. 28	The house is in 8th position from the left, which means there must be seven houses to the left of it. The house is in 21st position from the right, meaning there must be twenty houses to the right of it. Adding together the seven houses to the left, the twenty houses to the right, and the house itself, totals 28 houses altogether.
38.	B. 5	The letters and numbers relate to each other in terms of position. So if BALL = 1233, 1 = B, 2 = A and 3 = L. This is confirmed by the word WHALE being represented by 45236, where 2 represents the letter A once again, and 3 the letter L. In addition, the word WHALE shows that W = 4, H = 5, and E = 6. The first letter in the word HOUSE is H, and the information we have gathered tells us that the number representing H in the code is 5.
39.	C.	It is important to note that a yellow face must share an edge with a red face. This will only be the case when net C is constructed. Constructing all other nets will result in the yellow face being on the opposite side of the cube to the red faces, with no shared edges.
40.	C. $268	The option with less than $300 where the middle digit is 6 and the last digit is 8 is option C.

NOTES

Did you complete all of the questions in this book? If you did, congratulations! Your hard work and dedication will give you the rewards you deserve. Let me know how you did. I look forward to hearing from you.

Learning never stops, so let's go. Let's go. Let's prep for PEP and life!

NOTES:

NOTES: